HOME
WITH THE
HEATHER

HOME WITH THE HEATHER

BY BUS FROM LONDON TO JOHN O'GROATS

Gertrude Leather and
John Parke

LONDON
IAN ALLAN LTD

First published 1986

ISBN 0 7110 1550 3

Published by Ian Allan Ltd, Shepperton, Surrey;
and printed by Ian Allan Printing Ltd at their works
at Coombelands in Runnymede, England

Part 1

At Hounslow garage Inspector White signs the schedule which accompanied Mrs Leather on her journey and provided documentary evidence. *Surrey Herald*

Northbound

Fig 1: The outward bound journey to John O'Groats.

Map labels (north to south):
John O'Groats
WICK
HELMSDALE
INVERGORDON
INVERNESS
AVIEMORE
BLAIR ATHOLL
PERTH
STIRLING
GLASGOW
ABINGDON
LOCKERBIE
CARLISLE
KESWICK
WINDERMERE
LANCASTER
PRESTON
MANCHESTER
BUXTON
DERBY
WALSALL
BIRMINGHAM
STRATFORD
OXFORD
MAIDENHEAD
SLOUGH
LONDON
HOUNSLOW

Chapter 1

It was pouring with rain when I washed up the teacups in the Kitchen-I-like-to-get-away-from in Redway Drive, Whitton, near Twickenham, Middlesex. My husband was in the North of England on business, and my 22-year old daughter on holiday in the Isle of Wight. It was August and holidays were in the air despite the rain.

So I set off in slacks, a light sweater and a tweed coat. A small borrowed rucksack contained toilet things and overnight clothes and a folded summer dress in case the sun came out. The only idea I had was to go west, and see how far I could get and I went by the easiest means of transport I know about . . . I went by bus.

Changing 17 times and spending £1 19s 6d on bus fares, I travelled from Twickenham to Lands End – 300 miles – on ordinary service buses . . . and put myself into the headlines. This was the way I went: Twickenham, Hounslow, Slough, Reading, Newbury, Andover (overnight stop at a cafe), Salisbury, Yeovil, Taunton, Honiton, Exeter, Plymouth and across the ferry to Torpoint, St Austell, Penzance and Lands End.

I love sitting on top of a bus, where I can look at people's front gardens. I find it agreeable too to travel slowly through the countryside, and meet people on their daily round, doing their shopping and chatting with them about what they do and think. Travelling in the ordinary buses the atmosphere I found was very different from the train or holiday coach. Usually, I was the only passenger on holiday, everyone else was just going about their everyday business and in doing so – showing me a little of their world.

It rained all the time, and the driver put on the heater so I could dry out. It was early on Sunday morning and I had caught the first bus out of Andover where I had stayed on the Saturday night, and we were travelling on towards Salisbury. The countryside was lovely but everything was very, very wet. The warmth of the heater was very acceptable. By the time I was dry, the bus had begun to fill up and I could see the spire of Salisbury Cathedral.

I continued to travel west by bus. I bought a snack lunch at Taunton bus station and caught the next bus for Honiton in Devon. At three in the afternoon I was waiting for the Exeter bus and chatting to a Devonshire woman in Honiton. The main road traffic was splashing through puddles in the road a few feet from us, and we went on chatting about shoes for a schoolboy as if we had known each other for years. She had a young son who was due to start *proper* school 'after the holidays'. I had tea in a Lyons teashop in Exeter, and spent about 10 minutes looking in the shop windows, then went back to the bus station for the next bus to Plymouth.

I had never seen so much of our countryside in one day in my life – for I was travelling from eight in the morning until ten at night. I felt I could not stop until the buses stopped, and I saw the moon over the sea in Cornwall before I gave up and started to look for somewhere to spend the night.

The third day saw me travelling right across Cornwall. When I tired of looking out of the bus window I would chat with the passengers on the bus. A fresh face and a fresh topic – through the little villages, round the narrow bends and away over the hills.

Penzance and Lands End! The double-decker I was on drew up on the rocky promontory, and turned round. I got out of the bus, sniffed the salt sea air and pulled out my camera to take a picture of the bus then returned to my seat.

'We don't go any farther Lady!' remarked the conductor.

'I'm glad you don't,' I said in reply – and then added quietly, 'I've come from London by buses like this.'

The conductor had not heard me for he took no notice. I took out my bus tickets and began to total them up. How much had my 'see-how-far-I-could-go-trip', cost me?

Ten pence for this one, 1s 8d for that, 2s 4d for the next . . . I delved into my handbag for a pencil and a scrap of paper to help me total up the collection. The conductor looked up from what he was doing, and glanced in my direction.

'*Where* did you say you had come from?' he queried as if he had only just heard me.

'I've come from Twickenham. Its about 10 miles this side of London,' I replied, trying not to sound too elated. 'Here are my bus tickets!'

The driver had joined the conductor for a rest on the end seat, and they were so obviously amazed at my apparent madness and they just looked at each other silently. 'I saw you taking a picture of the front of the bus. What did you do that for?' put in the driver while he was summing me up.

'Oh that's just a souvenir!' I said. 'It's got Lands End on the indicator board up top.' Then they laughed and we all talked together. It appeared that they had both been on the buses for many years and they had never met anyone who had done that before.

Come from London by bus!

They helped me total up my bus tickets. I had spent £1 19s 6d and had 17 tickets and an extra one, marked one penny (for the Torpoint ferry). They no longer thought I was mad, but instead, congratulated me as having done something they had never thought of. In a short time they were taking my picture in front of the bus, and I snapped one of them too, and we were exchanging addresses so that I could send them a picture.

Their comments had, however, got me thinking – to what extent was my journey unusual? I decided to find out. Back in Penzance I spoke to the inspector at the bus station who told me that he had never heard of anyone doing such a trip and suggested that I should tell the newspapers. He was most enthusiastic about it, so I decided to follow his advice. Over lunch I worded a suitable telegram giving my address as care of the Post Office at St Ives – a seaside spot nearby where I thought it would be pleasant to stay the night. I sent it off at two o'clock and then walked down the main street to find the bus stop for St Ives.

Soon I was in the charming little harbour watching the tiny boats bobbing up and down in the sea – the Atlantic Ocean. It had stopped raining and the afternoon sun was warm. The light was brilliant and the little place with seagulls on every chimney pot seemed particularly friendly. I left my roll of film at a chemist and enquired about a 'bed and breakfast' place for the night.

Despite the many holiday makers I was soon fixed up, at a guest house in Skidden Hill, so I left my rucksack behind a settee in the lounge, had a wash and tidy up and left to go for a walk along Porthmear sands. It took me ages to get to the beach not because it was difficult to find or a long way away but because I was so fascinated by the studio cottages, some pink washed with blue doors, others whitewashed and gay with flower boxes, that I just ambled around, dodging into the courtyards and up alleyways that looked inviting.

St Ives, I found, was the established resort of many artists and doors were open during the holiday season so that visitors could walk in and look around. I forgot about the beach, watching an artist who was drawing cats. He was using a stick of charcoal on paper that looked wet – or it had been washed over with grey watercolour paint. He shaded in the ears quickly with the edge of the charcoal then roughed in two mischievious looking eyes and a sweet furry pussy came to life before my eyes. He told me that cats are hard to draw, but he had two that he liked to draw from memory. They were kittens really, he added, but they were growing fast.

I walked into another studio where somebody was carving beautiful animals out of beech wood. (I hope I'm right about it being beech!) Another time I met a dear woman – also an artist – who was crippled with arthritis and yet managed to paint attractive flower pictures (Mrs Nightingale). Did I say it took me hours to get to the beach?

I wandered round the wharf taking snapshots of delighted mothers enjoying the sight of their youngsters paddling in the safe harbour. I watched a black cat skirting the waves on the shore, treading cautiously as though not wanting to get her feet wet but her intense concentrated observation made me think she was inspecting the prospect of a fish supper.

Finally a short walk took me across to the beautiful sands of Porthmear, where the Atlantic rollers break into a curtain of spray against the rocks.

The past three days had been full of wonder. The experience of travelling across England had been exhilarating and I looked out over the wide expanse of ocean with a feeling of deep content. It was not weather for sitting about so I walked along the sea shore and over the rocks and back into the street to make a call at the Post Office. Several hours had gone by since I had sent my telegram to a London daily newspaper asking if it was interested in my bus riding adventure.

Well, I think you know the rest. The newspaper *was* interested and asked me to phone it (reversing the charges) full details and a description of myself. The details of the bus journey were comparatively easy, but I found it difficult to describe myself truthfully. Housewife of 50 with one grown-up daughter living in a pleasant house in one of the outer suburbs of London – that was truthful enough but a bit bare! Height 5ft 4in, hair fair sounded like a check on my physical attributes and maybe helped the picture. I left the Post Office stimulated by the contact and encouragement, and set off through the town for a place in which to get a meal.

Next I found a delightful restaurant overlooking the harbour and enjoyed a very nice meal. Afterwards I strolled round the illuminated harbour again in the evening, watched the crowds easing their way through the narrow streets and listened to the bells from the Catholic church ringing out a musical welcome. I knew no one but felt as if I were among friends.

To bed and the sound of the seagulls wheeling in a spiral just above the bedroom window gave place to the stillness of a moonlit night. I awoke early, and repacked my rucksack tidily for the return journey home, then went down stairs to cornflakes and egg and bacon for breakfast. The room was full of people, four to a table and I took an empty chair that was wedged tightly against its neighbours. No one spoke – breakfast was an important meal for family people on holiday. They are probably spending the day on the beach and taking a picnic lunch.

Soon I was out looking for a certain newspaper. Would my story have been used? – And if so, what would it look like?

I bought the paper and turned the pages, slowly searching for an inch or two or print with my name in it. Suddenly some words I had been reading leapt up at me with a bang! Here it was – the story of my bus journey with HEADLINES AS BIG AS THAT. I just could not bear the excitement and weakly took a chair in the shop.

The story had been given a prominent place in the paper – seven inches of space – and there was even a little map of my route. In an effort to regain my composure, I bought three more copies of the paper, and a packet of newspaper wrappers – and half in explanation but mainly because I would have burst if I had not told someone I pointed out the article to the girl at the counter. She stared at me hard as I explained . . . After a moment of astonishment, she said, 'May I show this to the manager? I know he would be very interested.' 'Of course!' I replied, and sat down to continue my recovery.

The girl disappeared behind some panelling and soon returned with the manager. He introduced himself, and we had a chat. 'I know several people who would like to know of this,' he told me, and after a few minutes he phoned various telephone numbers and arranged for local news reporters to call on him.

The feeling of excitement stayed with me the whole day which turned out to be full of surprises.

At the chemist's shop where I had left my roll of film to be developed, the girl who took my name at the counter said, 'There's someone waiting to see you, Mrs Leather,' – and introduced a young man with a camera who asked if he could take my picture.

'How did you know I would be coming?' was my natural question. He explained that he had come from Penzance where he had interviewed the driver and conductor of the Lands End bus who had told him that I had taken snapshots of them and promised to send them copies quickly. After that it was simple, he said. All he had to do was to phone the chemists in St Ives until he found one with a customer by my name and be waiting when I came in.

I enjoyed his idea of it being 'simple!' First he had gone to Penzance to find the crew of the bus – who might have been anywhere between Penzance and Lands End and *then* he had to locate the chemist who had my roll of film – and then he had to find me. He

must have driven miles. 'All part of my job as a reporter,' he said.

'What if I had taken the film home to be developed?' I teased him.

'Ah, but you didn't,' was his answer.

So that was how I came to be photographed getting on a bus for the return journey home. There was a soft mist over the harbour and I joined the queue in a drizzle but it turned out to be an excellent photograph – a real souvenir of my 300-mile bus ride and which I treasure.

At that moment the return journey represented another 300 miles, but I travelled back across England in the same way – by service bus and so made it 600 miles in all. The rain continued most of the way and at one time we appeared to be travelling through a double rainbow, surely a happy omen.

On the return journey I made an overnight stop at Exeter, where I got off the bus in a cloudburst, and again in Salisbury it was raining hard when I left the bus station to find my bed and breakfast accommodation for the night. Between the showers the sun would shine on a beautifully green English countryside. Even in the rain there was plenty to see – the patient cattle taking shelter under the hedges and the reflection of a rainbow in a village pond. Pots of gold, they tell me, can be found at the rainbow's end, but there was more comfort to me – being dry on the top of a bus – to have the rainbow itself.

It was surely the wettest holiday month we have ever known, August 1954.

Wiltshire, Dorset, Hampshire, Berkshire – changing buses at every town. During the three days travelling. It seemed like a grand rest and I enjoyed it all – another 300 miles through beautiful Britain. I had only to exert myself occasionally to get off the bus – to get a light meal when I could, and to get on another bus. Combined with the exhilaration and delight of the adventure it made a quiet holiday into something memorable. By the end of the third day from St Ives I was back home – not in the least tired but really refreshed by my unusual journey through the countryside.

Further surprises awaited me. There were letters and messages from people who had called to see me. I had thought my adventure was over, but it had really just begun. Among the letters, was a request to speak at a women's meeting and an invitation to the Silver Jubilee celebrations of the Omnibus Society – and to be a guest of honour at the society's dinner. Reporters who had called to see me before I arrived came again later, and I was scarcely able to keep up with the letters.

From the enthusiasm shown by members of the public who had read of my long distance ride by ordinary service buses I decided there would be sufficient support to run a Bus Riders Club so I suggested the idea to a reporter who thought it was excellent.

Finally a reporter called from a woman's magazine. The story was just what she wanted for *her* page, the sort of thing other women would be interested in. Would I give her more details – why I went – what I took with me – how much I spent on food – whom did I meet on the way . . . and last, but by no means least – where was I going to next? We kept up an enthusiastic conversation over tea and biscuits, while she jotted down what she wanted to know.

Then she rose to go, 'I've enjoyed talking to you so very much,' she said. Still talking at the front door she repeated . . . 'But you haven't told me where you are going to next?'

'I'll be off to John O'Groats!' I said.

Chapter 2

I thought no more about it.

The weather was getting very cold and my husband came home ill. I had plenty to do at home and all thought of holidays went out of my mind. But the letters continued to come in and in order to be able to give people the information they asked for, I had to have bus timetables. This was where the idea of the Bus Riders Club stood me in good stead. I found that when I sent for information about buses as an individual, I met with very little response and quite often the leaflets that were sent to me were about 'coach' tours. No one seemed to believe that I was asking for the ordinary local bus timetables.

As I came to realise this and asked on behalf of other people for what I wanted, the situation began to change, and the information came in with timetables, bus schedules, routes and town maps etc, until I was getting every possible kind of help from the omnibus companies all over the country. In this way, I began to build up an information library and I cleared shelf space as necessary to hold the books and map material. The replies I received were friendly and where the bus companies could give me additional help in the way of a link up with other bus routes they did so.

I was learning something fresh every day, and the idea grew. Each morning there were letters in the post – some from as far away as Australia – and each morning without fail I would answer them. Monday – usually such a humdrum day in a suburban home – took on a special delight, for there were always more letters.

So I settled down to organising a club which grew out of the letters I received and the questions I was asked. Some people seemed to write because they were lonely, others because they wanted to congratulate me on my 'courage' and because they too wanted to get out into the country and take a long bus ride to freedom. People overseas wrote when they were planning to come home on leave or because they just liked to correspond with someone in England. Whatever their reason – their sincerity demanded respect and attention and the letters were answered as fully as possible.

In a short time the Bus Riders Club had its own badge, designed by Mr Woods of Richmond, Surrey, from a suggestion I gave to him. A bright red silk pennant flag was produced by the silkscreen process by Mr Clarke of Twickenham and we had our own notepaper. After getting several estimates for printing on the writing paper, I thought that as we should need so much a small printing outfit would be an economy. So, while doing the shopping one weekend I chose a small Adana printing machine, and left the firm to add whatever accessories would be needed. They sent a little booklet along with the type and printing ink, and I set about learning to print. This took a lot of patience and I practised for several days. Ink and paper were lavishly wasted but within a few days I was satisfied with the result. Just before Christmas I printed over a hundred Christmas cards to send to members and friends. I was very glad that I did this as so many people sent Christmas cards to me that I would have felt embarrassed if I had not thought of doing this in good time.

About this time, I had another new experience – I gave a talk on my bus ride to Lands End in a church hall at Malden near Wimbledon. I bought a new hat for the occasion (as hats were being worn then) one of soft grey-green feathers to give me confidence (very necessary too!) for as I stood up to speak my hands went cold and my tongue, dry! The audience was composed of housewives like myself and they were so obviously attentive and interested that, after the first awful moment or two, I quickly felt at ease and the 'talk' gave way to a friendly 'chat' and was a great success. I took with me my collection of bus tickets and a diagram I made showing the route down through the west country, and it all helped to make the talk enjoyable.

A cold wet winter was followed by a chilly wet spring and by the time the sun came out, my daughter Ann was planning her wedding. We were fortunate in having a really lovely day for the wedding and she looked radiant in a picture dress of ivory silk embroidered with flowers and lovers' knots, and wore a charming head-dress that looked lovely over her fair hair. We had a delightful reception and there was a room full of wedding presents on view. The bridegroom and his friends took charge of the occasion and my husband was pleased that all his five brothers could get to the ceremony.

As you may guess all this excitement took my mind off bus riding but during the winter months I had completed as far as I was able, my collection of bus timetables – but there were so many of them that it was quite impossible that I had them all.

The letters from people interested in getting about in this way eased off during January and February but there was a sudden fresh interest again in March due to the appearance of the article by the woman reporter I mentioned earlier. Among these letters were several from women who asked if they could join the Bus Riders Club and accompany me on my ride to John O'Groats.

They took my breath away!

It was fantastic. At the time I had been excited and spoke without thinking – almost as a joke! You probably could not get to John O'Groats anyway. Surely they did not expect . . .

But it was obvious that they did expect me to carry out my idea of travelling across the country by buses. I had only myself to blame and there was no doubt in my mind that I should have to keep my word, but I parried the question for a while. It was too early – and I had no definite plans.

The questions came in thick and fast, 'How was I going?', 'When?' and I decided to organise a route. I would choose the prettiest way – through the little villages and through the holiday resorts. It would be a wonderful opportunity to see northern England, and Scotland – and incidently to check my own theories about bus riding being a good way to spend a touring holiday.

I knew southern England fairly well but not the area around Oxford and Stratford-on-Avon. This would be the first thing to find out and the first places to visit. I wanted to avoid the industrial Midlands and go slightly westward to take in the Thames Valley. There would be Maidenhead, Pangbourne, Sonning – all the pleasant riverside backwaters that I had read about.

The route map was found and placed where I could see it, I like to know the names and memorise the distances. Familiarity with the names of places takes away the feeling of knowing nothing about them. At Oxford the route would turn north towards Stratford-on-Avon, another unfamiliar place I should like to see. Up through Warwick to Birmingham with a view to seeing the beauty spots of Matlock and the Peak District.

Then on to Manchester and Preston to get to the beautiful scenery of the Lake District. I should certainly want to stop around Windermere . . . and see Wordsworth's home at Dove Cottage. I should have to find out exactly where that was.

So I worked at my programme – with route maps

and timetables around me. Keswick to Carlisle – that sounded fairly easy but after that, I drew a blank. How to get across Scotland?

Of course I'd never been to Scotland at all – so the place was a mystery to me . . . I shelved the problem for a few days while I studied the maps across England, and then I wrote to Stratford, Manchester, Preston and Keswick to get as many details as I could about the link-up of one company's buses with another. I knew it would be difficult for me to get away before lunchtime whatever day of the week I should choose to start. There would be shopping to do, and a lunch to get and odd jobs to see to.

With this idea in mind, I felt I would be wise to make Birmingham my first overnight stop. This would be about 100 miles and sufficient travelling for the first day. An early start the following morning would probably ensure my getting to the Lake District for the second night . . . This was the way I worked it out. If I left on a Friday, I could expect to be in the Lake District for a rest and to give me time to see the places I should hope to visit – Windermere, Troutbeck, Ambleside etc.

But Scotland was another thing altogether. No matter what enquiries I made I could not find out what I wanted to know about Scotland. Should I go across to Newcastle and make for Edinburgh or go to Glasgow first and then make my way across to Stirling and Perth for Inverness? These were my problems!

I went to the library to borrow some books. These only served to confuse me although I found fascinating reading, I saw delightful pictures of lochs and glens, and I made a note of the places talked about. I simply must go there . . . and there and there! But some were on the west coast and some were on the east coast and I couldn't visit them all – I really had to go up the centre, so to speak.

Eventually I laid a ruler on the map from Glasgow to John O'Groats and marked off the important towns that were between the two, and just hoped that there were sufficient lochs and glens to be seen from the buses I could take.

Having decided that I could not settle upon a hard and fast route, I gathered up all the bus maps of Scotland that I had collected and kept them together with a thick elastic band – I should need them all! And then I noticed that the Highland Bus timetable – the one I should want for the very end of the journey was *very* thin. I looked at it afresh . . . There were obviously very few buses. Tuesdays only . . . Saturdays only . . . School days only . . . alternate Sundays!

My head was in a whirl! I should need to be lucky to reach such a remote destination without being stranded.

Well, you can't really cross a bridge until you come to it, so I just had to hope that I and the bridge would be going in the same direction.

The days were going by and suddenly it seemed to

be summer. I became very busy arranging schedules for members who were planning their holidays. Somebody wanted to cross Yorkshire, taking in Cleckheaton and Doncaster, another wanted to get from Coventry to Maidstone, a third wanted Fairlight Cove near Hastings.

I had occasion to go to Cambridge and Bedford and detoured around the lovely countryside, painted and made famous by the artist Constable – coming back through Ipswich I saw at close quarters the charm of Flatford Mill, the subject of the 'Hay Wain'. I looked upon this journey as a kind of 'practice run' for the longer trip to Scotland and back . . . a kind of rehearsal, in fact.

A housewife has no set holidays and it is natural to make the arrangements to fit in with the family, so as my newly-married daughter and her husband were fixing up their holiday at the end of July, I decided to make that my 'date' too. I made no plans about accommodation, I intended to take pot luck all the way. The end of July and the first week of August would be the worst possible time to take a chance on finding accommodation . . . but if I could do it, then others would feel that they could do the same.

Personally I do not think much of holidays when they have to be booked up in advance. The element of surprise and adventure is reduced to a minimum and with it goes the holiday spirit. These remarks naturally do not apply to the family holiday. With young children one would have to make sure of suitable accommodation and nothing could take away their spirit of holiday adventure and excitement!

What to take with me became my next problem. I should be away for a fortnight so I would need a change of clothing. Fortunately the weather was settled – the daily weather forecast said that everywhere would be sunny and warm.

I made myself a kind of knapsack of blue linen and lined it with a thin plastic material to make it waterproof, and added two plastic pockets for toilet articles. Before doing this I looked at those in the shops and decided against a manufactured one. Even empty, they were heavy and too elaborate and expensive for my purpose.

I laid out my clothes, and then removed anything I thought I could do without! The final selection was as follows:

Overnight articles . . . towel and toilet things; Summer dress . . . extra shoes; extra blouse . . . underwear and hankies.

When packed the bag weighed six pounds which seemed enough for me to carry. I also had a brown leather one for money, comb, fountain pen, camera etc. I added a bright red silk wallet for the maps and timetables. Bright red so that it would be conspicuous if I dropped it or left it on a bus. I marked the wallet with my name and address in white paint.

My idea of course was not to be overburdened with clothes – or thoughts of them. For the journey I would be wearing a white blouse with slacks and a short tweed coat – and a red cotton headscarf. I would wear tennis socks and fairly heavy walking shoes with the slacks but a pair of flat heeled shoes went into the bag to go with the summer dress.

I need something over my hair but am not keen on hats except for dressed up occasions so I favoured a pirate headscarf folded across in a triangle with the knot at the back of the head. This is tidy and comfortable and some protection against the wind and rain. These details may seem superfluous but many people have asked what I wore for my bus journeys.

The sun continued to shine brightly but at the last moment I pushed a woollen cardigan into the top of my bag . . . one could not be sure of the weather in the far north or where my bus wanderings would take me.

Sun glasses went into my shoulder bag with a lipstick and comb. I would at least be a civilised nomad.

I stuck a stamp on a letter to my husband to post on the way.

I was ready for the road.

Chapter 3

I was going tomorrow . . . Friday 22 July.

As a last minute thought I bought three films for my Brownie camera, and added these to my luggage; and posted a pound note and 20 cigarettes to myself – addressed to the Post Office at Wick in North Scotland (which is about 20 miles south of John O'Groats and the last town marked on the map).

This was just a bit of fun between myself and Miss Stacey who worked behind the counter at our own post office in Whitton, Middlesex where I live . . . and I added a Bus Rider Club pennant flag marked London to John O'Groats – which I promised her I would bring back. It would be my prize to myself for having had the patience to do the journey!

To prove that I had gone all the way by service buses I took a piece of white card – which I planned to make my diary and schedule, I intended to ask bus inspectors at each bus station or depot and conductors when I paid my fare if they would sign the schedule for me. It would be in the nature of a souvenir of the journey as well as a record of the cost.

Up at seven to an early cup of tea, and the usual morning jobs. Round to the High Street for the shopping and a 'Cheerio' to many of my friends who knew that I was going. Back to a light lunch and while preparing it, I cut a sandwich for a snack later. I did not take a Thermos flask, for although a cup of tea is often welcome the flask is awkward to carry and tends to become a nuisance. I relied on finding a hot drink when I wanted it, on the way.

By noon I was out of the house, and starting the brief two-minute walk to the first bus stop for the No 33 to Hounslow garage – a fourpenny fare. It seemed a strange way to start a journey to John O'Groats – 600 miles away – but it was to feel stranger still.

Inspector White at Hounslow garage signed my schedule at 12.35 and wished me luck on the journey and saw me on to the 81 bus for Slough.

This is familiar ground to me, being a local route of London Transport, and I did not take much notice of the points of interest. But you will probably like to know that it passed London Airport (Heathrow). All the well known 'Airways' offices front the main road

for a mile or two and passengers can see the airliners take off from the tarmac runways from their point of vantage on the top of the bus.

From here I had seen a young couple off to Canada one evening. They left at 8pm and arrived at Goose Bay on the Hudson River in Canada for an 8 o'clock breakfast. I saw a plane like the one they had flown in, float off into the air as I passed . . . the modern way of travelling, no doubt . . . but I think I was equally thrilled with the adventure of my own way of getting about.

The faster you travel the less you see. Travelling at a high speed you miss the adventure of travelling.

I was relaxing gently after the excitement of getting away, ready to enjoy the experience of going so far by bus. Even the sunlight and shadow of the trees at Colnbrook, an idle observation of that little backwater village, gave me pleasure.

Arriving at Slough at 10 minutes past one, I was soon on the next bus for Maidenhead. I had passed north of Windsor and Eton in the Thames Valley and at Maidenhead the main road goes over the River Thames. It is a delightful spot, one well placed for the millions of Londoners who must go there through the year to spend their leisure hours by the river.

As a contrast to the airport traffic I had seen an hour ago I was now taking interest in some of the old coaching inns that remain on this road – delightful places still with sloping roofs and oak-beamed rafters. I saw old beehives under the trees in an orchard and quaint little houses that turned their backs to the road.

I was in London's country – the green belt, part of the open country which stretches for miles round the city. It took me until 2.15 to get to Maidenhead and my schedule (or log) was signed by Mr Chapman, the conductor. Littlewick Green, Twyford and Sonning, I was travelling a long road with a light heart. The highway appeared to flow between the fields on to Reading where I arrived at half past three. There was half an hour to wait so I filled in the time by having a cup of tea and a sandwich at a nearby cafe. I left Reading at 4pm for Oxford to continue along the Thames Valley. For part of the way the road runs along

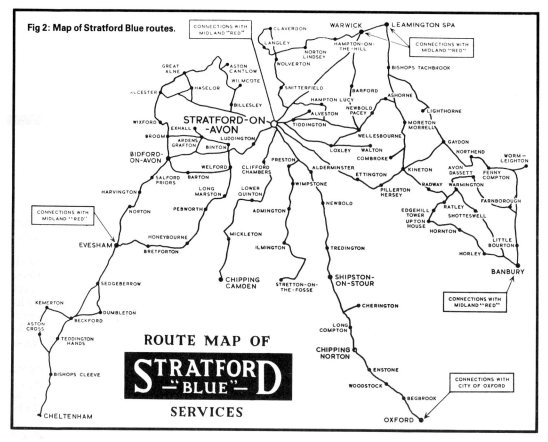

Fig 2: Map of Stratford Blue routes.

ROUTE MAP OF
STRATFORD "BLUE"
SERVICES

the river, wide and calm. Away on the other side the tall grasses bend gently in the breeze. I caught a glimpse of a brown mallard duck skimming over the water.

Pangbourne, Streatley, Goring and Moulsford and on to Wallingford, a lovely market town with an old-English air about it. The marketplace was busy with shoppers and the bus waited there for several minutes before continuing the journey.

I arrived at Oxford just before six o'clock with barely a minute to catch the bus for Stratford-on-Avon. The High Street was crammed with cars and bicycles and I thought I should miss the bus for we entered the town at a crawl. I know it well but just then I was feeling anxious about the possibility of losing my bus and the connection for Stratford-on-Avon is very 'tight'. I think there were only two minutes to spare and the bus was fairly full. Sometimes a connection like this looks alright on the timetable – but becomes very difficult to catch. It is impossible to snatch a cup of tea before the connecting bus is ready to move off.

On this occasion I put my knapsack on the bus and asked people nearby if they thought I would have time to get a bun?

'Good heavens, no', was the chorus. 'We're late already!' another said, 'we shall be off in a moment.'

So I found a seat and sat down but in next to no time my neighbour was delving into her bag and brought out some biscuits. We had a chat and I explained that I hoped to have time for some food and tea but 'the buses are too efficient' was the way I put it. This led to an amusing episode. She spoke to a young boy on the bus – Roger Thompson – who would have been about 10. 'Roger,' she said, 'you live the nearest to a bus stop. When you get off, you go and get the lady a drink, while I'll hold the bus up!'

Roger seemed quite willing to oblige and at Enstone on the other side of Woodstock, he dropped off the bus quickly and was away to the other side of the road, where he disappeared behind the village Post Office. The lady who had been talking to me kept an eye on Roger until he went out of sight – and then slowly oh so slowly, she gathered up her belongings, looked to see if she had her purse, and her shopping – shook hands with me, and wished me well and as Roger appeared with the drink by the step of the bus, handed it to me with a special smile and then got down from the bus! Thanks again for your friendliness and for the drink.

We had been passing through some of the prettiest villages I had ever seen – many with a village green and a duck pond beside the green. They are a sight to

14

see, a lovely touch of rural England. It was market garden country at first; opening up into larger fields and paddocks. Cows and calves moved shoulder to shoulder munching their way from one side to the other.

A farm girl in blue jeans and a shirt that exactly matched her tanned face noticed me studying the cows and remarked that they did better when they were reared close up to one another. I was not sure that I understood what she meant, but perhaps it was just that the animals liked company.

I looked up at a cat sitting high on a hay stack, and watched the animals as we passed them . . . horses, cows, calves, pigs and kittens! Sun, air and exercise – no wonder the animals looked beautiful. The weather was hot and sunny and I luxuriated in it from my vantage point on the bus.

We had passed close to Blenheim Palace near enough to get a glimpse through the trees – almost everyone on the bus craned their necks to look. These lovely places have a charm of their own, that can never be extinguished. Their associations too can never die. This was the ancestral home of the Marlborough family – the Churchills.

This was a long journey though delightful – two hours of bus riding from Oxford to Stratford on the Avon. We were travelling northwest, and by now I was about 70 miles away from London.

About half way we came to Chipping Norton, affectionately known there as 'Chippy.' Away to the west lay the Vale of Evesham and the stone-walled Cotswold road to Moreton-in-Marsh. There is something romantic and intriguing about the names of these places: reading a map becomes as much of a pleasure as reading a book. More so, too, as I was seeing so many of them.

I had been looking forward to seeing Stratford-on-Avon but I am afraid I was disappointed at what I could see from the bus as we drove in. I had expected to see old Elizabethan houses and kissing gates and twisted chimneys and little yew trees trimmed and cut like birds! Where did such a picture come from, in my mind? For what I actually saw were spacious roads and modern houses and the Shakespeare Theatre that was square and made of modern bricks.

This taught me a lesson. I had been thinking I had been travelling the open road with an open mind but I was wrong! I was bringing something with me that I did not need. It helped me to change my viewpoint and divest myself of my preconceived ideas and to realise again that the slower one travels, the more one sees, and that recollections like this are etched upon the mind for all time. I had the time for such experiences and enjoyed taking myself to bits in this way. It helped me to pass the time, and to 'set me right'.

By now I had eaten my sandwich and was terribly hungry, and could not wait to get off the bus to look for a meal. The only place I could see nearby was a cafe of the teenage type with people sitting outside at little tables. No matter, I was in a mood to enjoy anything and what an appetite I brought to the table!

The room was full – teenage cyclists mainly and we all sat together up at the counter. I had cheese and tomato sandwiches and two cups of coffee – then I bought a cake and some chocolate. It may not sound much but I feared that I might find nothing at all.

There was time to take a close look at the statue of Shakespeare by the bridge, and see the gardens, and go and have a wash and brush up, and then it was necessary to be looking our for my next bus – service No 150 for Birmingham. The time was nine o'clock and it was beginning to get dark as I boarded the bus but I should be in the heart of the Midlands before nightfall. Travelling alone as I do I never anticipate any problems with overnight stops.

From here we travelled through the heart of the Shakespeare country in the twilight. Bearley Cross to Wootton Wawen, Henley in Arden (we must be near the forest of Arden), Hockley Heath, Monkspath, Shirley and Hall Green.

My fare was 2s 6d and my schedule was signed by Mr John Goodman of the joint Midland Red and Stratford Blue service.

Soon after ten o'clock we pulled up by a church and I was in Birmingham. My first day's travelling was over – approximately 90 miles. As I got off the bus, I saw a policeman on the other side of the road, so I caught up with him and asked him if he could recommend a hotel for the night. He told me of two or three, so I went to the Arden – about five minutes' walk away. Soon I was having tea and biscuits in the lounge before going to bed . . . I asked to be called early; then slept like a log.

Chapter 4

Birmingham was busy when I left in the morning after a light breakfast. I threaded my way through the streets to the Midland Red bus stop. There were queues everywhere as it was the Saturday morning before the bank holiday week and thousands would be on holiday. The bus I wanted was the one for Derby, leaving at eight o'clock. If I made sure of this, I had good hopes of being in the Lake District for the night – a journey of something like 150 odd miles.

It was a beautiful morning, bright and sunny but a little chilly at that hour, as I stood in the queue. The bus left with a full load and went via Chester Road, Sutton Coldfield, Mere Green, Lichfield and Burton on Trent, and we arrived at Derby soon after 10 o'clock.

This was a lovely run and I was particularly charmed with what I saw of Derby. The roads were wide and there were pleasant houses and pretty gardens for miles of the way. I talked with a friendly woman on the bus who told me that she had lived at Nuneateon as a child and that a visit to Derby had always been looked upon as a 'real holiday outing'. She told me about the Grand Union Canal which meant as much to them as the River Thames does to the Londoner and how all the goods used to be transported by the canal barges.

The fare for this journey was 3s 10d and I have the signature of Mr S. Evans on the schedule.

Arriving in Derby I lost no time in finding the next bus, the one to take me on to Buxton . . . due out of Derby at 10.35am. This was another long run, through all the High Peak and Matlock neighbourhood – well known and much loved holiday places for many people from the Midlands and north of England, and I enjoyed it immensely.

The bus stopped everywhere along the route. I became fascinated to know just how often we stopped – so I counted the halts and made a note of it. (We stopped 30 times in the two-hour journey.) I never became bored for there was so much to see. We went via Duffield, Belper, High Peak (the highest spot around), Matlock Bath, Darley Dale, Haddon Hall, Bakewell and Topley Pike, reaching the market place at Buxton at 12.54.

I particularly enjoyed the scenery around Matlock, and the long hill climb into Buxton. I noticed how the driver kept changing his gears as we made height.

Stone walls now lined the roads instead of hedges, and stone is used a good deal for the houses. It gives the scene a much more rugged look. My neighbour pointed out the local beauty spots, and the caves where people go to see the stalagmites and stalactites. I was charmed by her Derbyshire dialect which was sweet and friendly.

Then a strange thing happened. The bus stopped and the lady said goodbye and she left. Another took her seat, a woman who had been sitting behind me. She began to point out things, just as the former one had done and made slight sounds – as if it was an effort to talk. She smiled and frowned and gesticulated, and I realised that she was dumb, but wanted to show me the sights, in the same way that the other had been doing! This was awkward, but then I remembered that I had two photographs of myself and some newspaper cuttings with me.

I got them out of my bag and showed them to her, and pointed to myself and to the picture – saying this is ME!

Her eyes lit up with obvious pleasure, and turning round to the seat behind her conveyed to her friends something about me in deaf and dumb signs, which of course, I did not understand. They laughed and made signs, and shook me by the hand. Obviously they wanted to congratulate me and wish me luck! They were so *very* pleased that we understood each other. I thought that they looked happy and were probably on holiday, judging from their clothes and demeanour.

Quite soon they had gone, and I was on my own again. We passed close by Haddon Hall, and I caught a glimpse of Baslow. The road was quiet and the countryside looked peaceful in the noonday sunshine.

I was glad of my sunglasses, as without them I would have noticed the glare from the road. We pulled right up against the stalls in the Market Place in Buxton, and I noticed several hikers clad in shorts and waterproof jackets among the people. They carried enormous packs on their backs and looked as if they

Fig 3: Map of Midland Red Services.

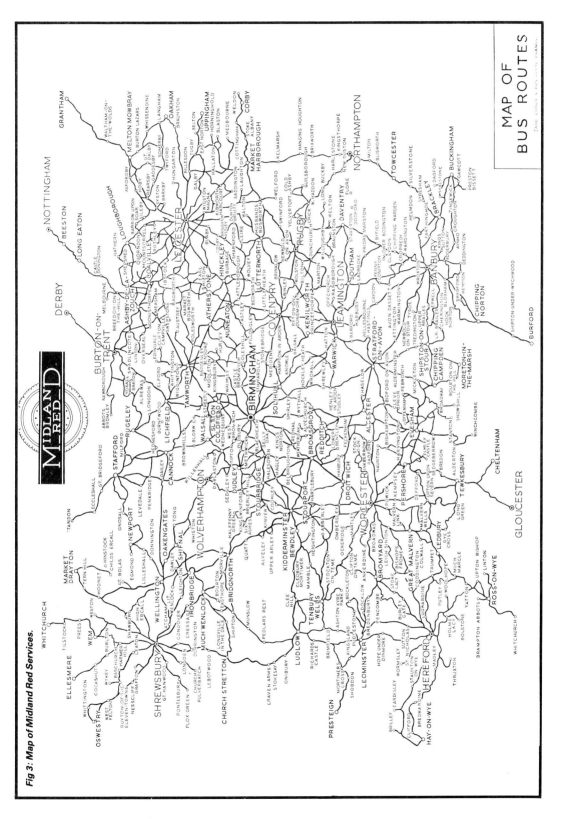

MAP OF
BUS ROUTES

17

might be campers and have blankets rolled up with their things. They certainly were having wonderful weather for whatever it was they were doing.

My hopes of a 'proper' lunch disappeared with the sight of the Manchester bus already drawn up nearby. It was due out at 1.18, so I had about 20 minutes to spare.

I crossed the market place to a cafe in expectation of getting at least a sandwich. It was quite full with several people standing around the doorway. I had to make do with an ice cream if I intended to get the bus. There would not be time to search around.

I had set my heart on sleeping somewhere in the Lake District otherwise I should not have minded the thought of missing the bus. I took the ice cream and found myself a seat on the bus. I wished I could have met one of those people who arrange these timetables . . . as I have remarked already, it looked all right on paper.

I tucked the Derby to Buxton 4s 6d ticket into the rubber band with the others, and folded the schedule away temporarily. It now had another signature on it, Mr M. R. Walker, conductor for North Western Road Car Co. Everyone was accepting the idea of my schedule in good humour, and of course, I only had to mention that I was on my way to John O'Groats in buses like these to start a friendly chat.

We went to Manchester by the Long Hill route, and in lieu of a meal, I had a doze.

The sun had given my arm nearest the window quite a pleasing tan by the time I woke up and we were running into the outskirts of the town. We were due in at about 3.10pm. The fare for the single ticket was 3s 2d, and the log for the journey was initialled N.G.R. I had been to Manchester once before and this time I would know where I was in relation to the shops and the centre of the town when I got out of the bus.

At Manchester there were plenty of buses going my way, so I decided I would have time for a look around the city, and make sure of something to eat. A few minutes walk – it was nice to stretch my legs – brought me alongside the Midland Hotel and into the square, where I found a cafe which could provide eggs on toast, tea and cakes and made up for the lost lunch. I also bought a piece of cake and a slab of whole nut chocolate – to guard against further emergencies! Wrapped up securely, they were pushed into one of the plastic pockets of my knapsack. I looked around a few shop windows then made my way towards the bus station for a bus going to Preston.

Enquiries led me to taking the next Blackpool bus which would stop at Preston, and thereby get me over another 20 miles or so. This left Manchester at 4.45pm and we had not been going for more than a quarter of an hour before we had to pull in a little to allow a fire engine to pass.

Excitement for a few minutes! I noted the time – 5pm – and the place – Salford – and wondered what it was. But I shall never know! All we could see from the top of the bus were hoses, firemen, smoke and engines and a small crowd of people. It was in a turning to the left of the main road going through Salford . . . and there was a lot of smoke. Maybe a warehouse was burning or it might have been a shop.

Settling back into my seat after seeing the fire, there was another diversion in the form of a lorry that had shifted its load. It was drawn into the curb, and the load which looked like wholesale size cartons of washing powder was hanging off in a perilous position. Another lorry driver was helping with the dismantling of the cargo, so that it could be righted.

I had entered into conversation with my seat companion – a girl nearest me, and a young man next to her. I was highly entertained by their talk. There is something about the local dialect which reminds me of a comedy act, probably because so many of the famous comedians come from the north that I was prepared to laugh at anything.

'You tell her! You tell her!' nudged the girl to her companion. He was obviously shy of 'telling' what it was, so she began the story for him.

'You remember . . . it was when the boilers broke down, and you' . . . she insisted.

'All right, I'll tell her,' said the gentleman and he began his tale with many promptings from the lady on my right.

'You see, the boilers had to be stopped . . . the fires put out, and we were ''Laid off'' for 10 weeks. I had 30 shillings to my name, and I hitch-hiked all across France, then up through Belgium into Holland getting odd jobs.'

'And you came back with 30 *pounds*. That was before we got married,' the girl reminded him.

'Yes that's right! I ended up with the easiest job of the lot. Picking and packing tulips. You can only hold four in your hand at a time. Mustn't hold 'em! Bea-u-tiful job if you know the ropes. Easiest money I've ever earned.' He laughed heartily at his own recollections.

He spoke with animation and gestures so that I could understand what he meant. How gently he picked those tulips and how tenderly they were laid in the packing boxes. He threw out his arm wide to the windows of the bus, and I caught a glimpse of the acres of tulips – 'pink, white, mauve, some almost black they were so dark, lovely pinks and reds . . . ' the Dutch bulbfields came to life as he talked. 'They had to eat them during the war, y'know . . . the bulbs – they stewed them and fried them, and they didn't do them much good . . . tummy pains . . . ugh! They are all right again now. You ought to see those beautiful tulips. They're real grand,' he added. His eyes shone.

He talked so quickly that I could not be sure he meant the flowers, the bulbs or the Dutch people. He was so enthusiastic that I gathered he admired them all.

We exchanged names and addresses and I promised to let them know whether I reached John O'Groats safely . . . and I wrote to them later, Mr and Mrs H. of Garstang near Preston.

In a while they were gone, and I was on my own again, with the bus running into one of the bus stations at Preston. This was six o'clock on Saturday and Preston was a mass of buses. They seemed to be going everywhere. This was a big junction for East Lancashire and thousands of people use it for Morecambe and Blackpool.

I wanted to go north to Lancaster and after making enquiries decided that I would have time for a cup of tea and a sandwich.

My schedule, by the way, for this last journey was initialled J. B. (Ribble), and the fare from Manchester to Preston on this route was 3s 6d.

I took one or two snapshots of the buses for my album, and wandered out into the nearest road for a little walk and a peep at the shops before returning to the bus station for my bus to Lancaster. The crowds had thinned a little and I got a seat up top, and near the front for another hour's travelling.

I think I must have dozed on this bus, for I scarcely remember anything about it, yet my schedule is signed and I have a ticket which cost 1s 9d, so I stayed awake long enough to pay my fare. I had been on buses since eight o'clock in the morning since I left Birmingham so there is some excuse!

I had to have my wits about me when I arrived in the bus station at Lancaster for the next bus I wanted was actually on the move. Fortunately I had explained to the conductor that I had hoped to get on to Windermere and he made signs to the driver of the 8.28 to stop for me. My schedule was signed by W. N. D. at 8.25pm (Lancaster) and the next entry was Lancaster to Windermere for 8.18 . . . 10.03pm signed by H. B. Cartland.

I think I was lucky. It looks as if the bus was late getting away from the bus station or I would have missed it. This was a double-decker, and the fare to Kendal was 2s 1d. At first I did not realise that it would be going right through to Windermere, and that I need not change again, but such was the case so I paid another 10d for the rest of the journey. Just before we reached Windermere, we passed a delightful topiary garden. Every little tree was shaped and trimmed, some into spirals and others like birds – it may have been a nursery garden devoted to these unusual trees.

There was a simplicity and dignity about them that was most artistic. I could imagine the gardeners working out this technique of trimming until a flawless arrangement was achieved. It was a most unusual sight.

I was due at Windermere at 10.03pm – I found that the buses were making me 'time conscious'!

I had passed quite close to Morecambe Bay, and caught a glimpse of the sea and noted with pleasure the distant hills of Cumberland to the north. As we went through the town of Kendal and pulled away up the hill

to the left fork, I saw the heavy lorries turning away to the right. The conductor, to whom I had been talking, told me that they drive over the heights of Shap Fell on their way to Scotland, roads that are often impassable during the winter owing to snow drifts. He told me about the 'Eagles Nest' on the road to Penrith – a rendezvous where the eight-wheel lorries can pull up, so that the drivers can have a rest before continuing the climb.

This was my last bus journey for the day, and we reached Windermere station to time.

I got off the bus and shouldered my knapsack and swung off with a light-hearted step down the road. The moon was coming up, and I though I would like to see the moon over the lake before finding myself a room for the night. I had a vague idea of finding Lake Windermere 'just around the corner'. After walking briskly for about 10 minutes and finding myself still among the trees and houses, and still going downhill, I decided to ask.

I got a shock when I was told that it was about a 1½ miles away, and that the place I must have in mind was Bowness-on-Windermere. I discovered later that what I really expected to find was the pier at Waterhead, and that I should have stayed on the bus for another five minutes or so.

It was a really beautiful night. There was a full harvest moon ahead of me and the scent of pine trees all round – so I walked on, down, down into Bowness, and round the bend by the church until finally I was beside the lake.

And what a sight met my eyes. The reflection of the moon rippled to meet me over the water. The distant trees and hills were silhouetted against a jade and purple sky. From a nearby garden I caught a pungent whiff of tobacco flowers and water, rock and moonbeams mingled with the magic of the night air to make it unforgettable – I was unwilling to leave such a scene.

I saw a few pebbles scattered round the base of an upturned boat, and picked one up to throw into the water, just to see the calm surface break into ripples . . . my rendezvous with the magic of the evening was over.

I turned away, in the direction of the nearest hotel. 'Sorry, we're full up . . .'

'No, I'm sorry . . . '

'I'm *very* sorry but . . . '

I thought of the benches on the promenade overlooking the lake. Nothing could have been more tempting at that moment. Just by the church I saw the familiar form of a policemen. I asked him whether he thought I would be likely to get fixed up anywhere for the night.

'You'd be *lucky* – I've never seen the place so full.'

'In that case,' I pointed to where the benches were just a little way away, 'I think I'll sit down there if that's all right.'

'You'll be in good company,' was his good-natured

reply.

But I was luckier still.

A lady who had heard me making enquiries and saw me speaking to the policeman came over to me and told me of a friend of hers, nearby . . .

The rising moon spread a path for me over the limestone rock of a lakeside garden, so I followed the woman towards a cottage. Inside the atmosphere was friendly in spite of the hour, and I was soon settled for the night with Mrs Dent.

Chapter 5

Any lover of sunshine, bird song and water pictures would have enjoyed being in Bowness that morning.

It was Sunday, and there was no need to hurry. I had planned on an easy day, so I stayed awhile talking to Mrs Dent. We walked together down by the lake and took several pictures of each other to keep for souvenirs, and when I left – at about 11 o'clock, she came up the winding street with me to the bus stop.

'Au revoir,' we said, hoping to meet again someday, and she wished me luck on my journey. This bus took me back to Windermere station – the mile or two I had walked downhill the night before.

While waiting for the bus to take me to Ambleside, I reviewed my position. London was about 260 miles away, and soon I would be in the heart of the Lake District . . . Ambleside, I think, is the recognised 'centre', and this was only five miles away. Here the hikers congregate for the climb up Helvellyn, and gather for coffee and to buy postcards of the beauty spots around. Keswick was 16 miles to the north, on Derwentwater and the high fells and forests of Cumberland stretched away to the north-east.

I could not hope to go climbing, but I expected to have the opportunity of seeing Grasmere and the Cumbrian mountains from the top of the bus. I was not disappointed – in a quarter of an hour after boarding the bus, I was in Ambleside, having passed Troutbeck bridge and the Waterhead Pier for Windermere Lake steamers on the way.

This, by the way, is the point where the bus stop is within a few hundred yards of the lake and where I should have alighted the night before. It was a small error of judgment on my part and was not important.

At the Ribble bus station in Ambleside I pushed my knapsack over the counter, paid for the ticket and got rid of it for a few hours while I had lunch and looked around. I would have to leave for the north from this point later on – so there was no need for me to take my luggage around with me. The left luggage office was piled up high with massive grey-green rucksacks, the kind that are built on a bamboo frame. A group of boys in corduroy shorts and green windcheaters had just left the office and were sunning themselves on the low wall

of the bus depot . . . no doubt they had the same idea.

I walked downhill first, just to look at the shopping area and then retraced my steps past the bus depot to look for a cafe for lunch. I found a very nicely-cooked meal at 'Peggy's Cafe' and then went for a short walk to see the tiny house that had been built on a stone bridge over a stream, known as Bridge House. It functioned as an antique shop. I sat up on the bridge coping for a while with a party of girl cyclists. They were mostly in blue jeans and wore coloured sweaters.

'I'm hoping to get a copper-beech tan like yours!' I said to them enviously.

'Oh, we tan without a struggle especially at mountain height,' replied one of them.

'What do you do when you're not cycling?' I asked.

'We climb and swim in the lake when we feel energetic enough, otherwise we just laze around,' was the carefree reply.

We talked for a time, and then I left them and made my way down to the edge of the lake. I could see the steamer leaving Waterhead Pier in the distance, while near me at the water's edge crowds of happy children were paddling and playing.

I found two small children behind a large boulder who seemed to be in trouble. I could hear them from where I sat, one was crying and the other, obviously the older of the two who had taken control of the situation was 'trying to do something about it!' I walked to the top of the boulder and looked down on the little mites who at first glance appeared to be in swimming suits. Then I saw that the smaller one who was coughing and crying at the same time was without any.

'What's the trouble?' I asked, pleasantly enough.

Two little frames shuddered with shock at my sudden appearance. They were cold and miserable. I didn't think I looked as bad as all that, but perhaps I seemed like the voice of authority to them!

'Its Iris . . . she's been in the water . . . and she shouldn't have. She was wearing Tony's costume . . . It was too big . . .'

The story was poignantly brief and to the point.

'Well, don't cry. It will be alright.' I attempted to

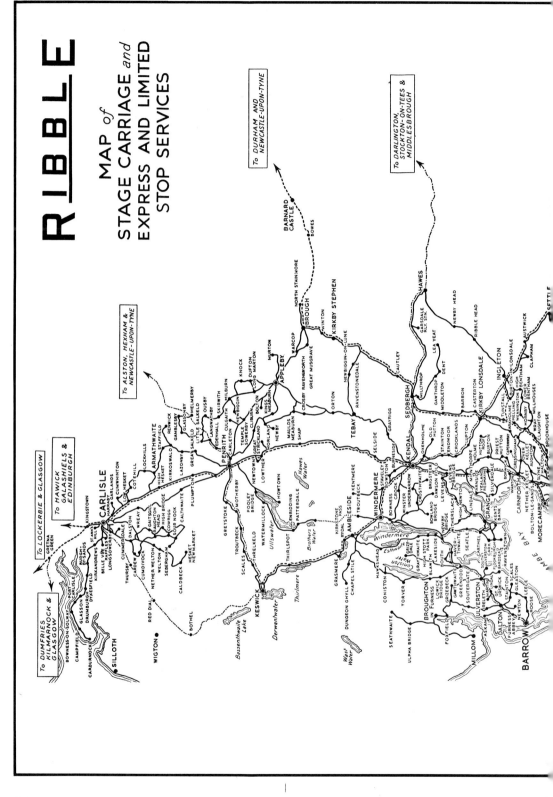

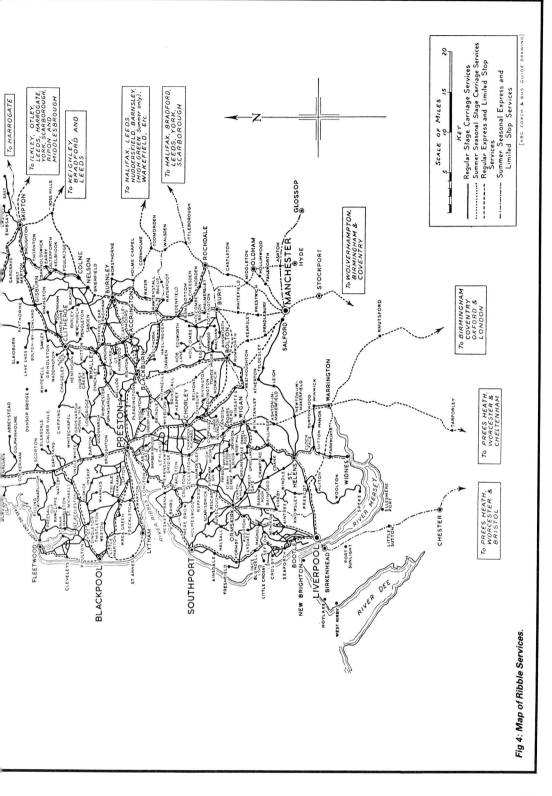

Fig 4: Map of Ribble Services.

soothe her and climbed down the rocks to be nearer their level.

'She can't go back like that, can she?' and then to Iris. 'You CAN'T go back like *that!*'

I tried a little chatter as a preliminary course. 'You look nice and brown. How old are you Iris?' I asked her touching the young lady's tresses.

I should have known better, we were hardly acquainted.

I'm seven and Iris will soon be five!' The answer came from the other while Iris offered a fresh shower of tears.

'Perhaps I can find your mother,' I suggested, No, this was no good – they would get into trouble because they had been warned not to go in the water.

'Haven't you any clothes?'

'No, they were with Mum.'

'A towel perhaps!'

'No.'

Well, I knew where to get a towel, having brought one with me, wrapped up with my own swimming costume. It was but a short climb over the rocks and I returned with it. I also found a couple of safety pins in my handbag. No embroidered dance frock could have been more acceptable than the princess negligee we designed for Iris that afternoon. She grinned with satisfaction as I looked for a stick with which to go fishing for the missing garment in the Lake.

When I came back they were jumping up and down, laughing merrily for I held the dripping thing away from me, acted up a bit.

'Is this the *treasure*?' I called out. We squeezed the water out of it between us, all three of us working hard to make it as dry as possible.

'Now, when you've got it on, you've got to run like mad and get yourself dried and dressed. Promise!'

Iris promised and my emergency bar of chocolate went. We helped each other up the rocks and they left me both running hard across the grass. I saw them disappear into the picnic crowds gathered near the beech trees.

I rolled up a damp towel with a dry swimming suit and turned in the opposite direction. It was nearly teatime, so I went back to the cafe where I had a 'high' tea.

A sightseeing tour of Grasmere with a visit to Wordsworth's Dove Cottage and the churchyard where he was buried came next. A sixpenny bus ticket would take you into Grasmere from Ambleside, and you get a truly magnificent view from the top of the bus.

I almost forgot to mention that Dove Cottage is almost hidden from view up a little lane at Rydal Mount, near Grasmere. There are tiny windows and narrow doors and the interior is of dark oak panelling. There are charming little alcoves in this little cottage where Wordsworth lived with his wife Mary and sister Dorothy.

Only a few people are able to get in the rooms at a time; but I was able to see the desk where he wrote some of the finest poetry in the English language. He was made Poet Laureate in 1843.

Outside there is a tiny patch of garden sloping up to the hills beyond. I was advised where to go to see it and it was well worth a visit.

In this way I saw as much as I could of Grasmere and Rydal Water before returning to Ambleside in the early evening. Campers were pitching tents and settling down for the night as I passed close by on the bus and picnic parties were gathering up their belongings and preparing to leave.

It had been a wonderful day and everywhere the scenery had been breathtaking. The moon was coming up over Loughrigg and I thought I would have another short walk beside Lake Windermere before nightfall.

The steamer alongside the pier was bringing in the last load of passengers and the boatmen were relaxing after a busy day. I found a place on the bank for a quiet half hour and from somewhere behind me I could hear the merest whisper of a song. The sound came probably from a portable radio – or from a car but no matter, they added a sentimental background to the scene. I stayed beside the water watching a feathery veil of mist gather over the grasses in the distance and then reluctantly left. I made my way up a narrow path to an ivy-clad, mellow old house which I had noticed was a guest house called Ghyll Head, where I was fortunate in finding some supper and a comfortable bed for the night.

Monday morning – up bright and early to look in at the Post Office at Ambleside before continuing my journey, and soon I was boarding the bus to Keswick. It was very full and the conductor was busy, so after chatting with my seat companion, I asked her if she would be kind enough to sign my schedule for me. She was Miss M. Green from Birmingham and was on holiday with a party of girls. She told me that she was a school teacher, and she was most interested in my journey. The whole party left the bus at the foot of Helvellyn to make the climb. I should think that it would have been a strenuous journey on such a warm day.

The mountain was in full sun over to my right and there seemed little shade on such a half-wild rock. To the other side of the bus lay Thirlmere, a narrow lake which runs for some good distance beside the road. Here were wooded glens and rocky banks planted with the smaller trees, birch, a good deal of mountain ash and holly, thorn and juniper; some of these had been allowed to seed and spring up in the rocky banks.

At one bus stop, I found myself looking down a little dell with a rock wall in half shadow from which had grown tiny hart's tongue fern and mosses. For a moment, I saw a distinct picture of cool blue-green herbs growing out of a miniature waterfall – and just as suddenly, it had gone.

I was fascinated too, by the old country dwellings by the roadsides. The main fabric was of near-at-hand material but if the cottage was a little above the road there would also be a bit of dry wall and rough steps made of the wide slabs of stone.

I noticed how smoothly they had worn with the years. The pinks, pansies and sweet williams of the cottage flower borders were never so lovely as when they hung in drifts over the edges of these stone paths.

I liked to see the woodland lanes, and trees meeting overhead so that the light coming through was dim and green. The most mysterious of all are the narrow tracks that pass through the woods of tall pines. There the trees stand thickly, nothing grows upon the ground, but where the firs are thinnest the bracken formed a green carpet underfoot. When the bus stopped near the trees, I noticed the strong smell of pine needles heated by the sun.

An hour passed and I was in Keswick on Derwentwater. I walked through the High Street among the hikers and found my way down to Friars Crag – the beauty spot that is known and loved by thousands.

I watched a fisherman cast his line into the water from a nearby boat and bring out a little 'fella' – quite five inches long. The man looked thoroughly satisfied.

I lunched at a restaurant near the Post Office, and made my way back to the bus depot to continue my journey to Carlisle. My schedule notes the important fact in red ink: *Dep. Keswick 1.40. R. H. Scott. Insp:* I was not quite out of the Lake District yet. Skiddaw lay over to the right and Bassenthwaite lake stretched for about five miles not far from the road but over on the left – to the west. We were now travelling northeast and soon I was the only passenger on the bus. I talked to the conductor, Mr B. M. Horner who signed my schedule and gave me my single ticket to Carlisle. We travelled by way of Bothel, Mealsgate and Thursby among the lovely farmsteads and quiet villages.

We were leaving the excitement and thrills of the Lakeside scenery and entering an entirely different kind of landscape. It was open country on both sides, stretching away for miles, but with the sunshine nothing could be dull. The harvest had been gathered in but the stubble was golden yellow and there were fluffy white clouds in the sky which suggested fine weather for the future.

Mr Horner was very helpful and advised me to go up to Scotland by way of Glasgow from Carlisle, and with him I built up some sort of plan of the rest of the journey. He suggested I should call in at the office of the Western (SMT) at Carlisle for details, but this was not necessary for I had its timetable with me. I enjoyed this part of the journey immensely. Here was peace, privacy and loveliness . . . we were away from the advertisement hoardings which so often disfigure the landscape near the cities. I looked into the homes of people who lived simple lives and enjoyed the quiet pleasures. Everything about these country homes was strong and serviceable, and looked as if it would wear for ever.

The bus pulled into Carlisle soon after 3pm. I walked out of the 'exit' and straight round to the 'entrance' side for the Glasgow bus. The time was 3.10pm. There was no sign of the bus so I enquired at the Western SMT office which is situated between the two bus garages. The girl at the counter told me that it would be leaving at that minute. The girl next to her said . . . 'I think it's just gone!' I had missed the Glasgow service bus by exactly *three* minutes. I was so disappointed, but was advised that there was a Ribble 30 service at 3.23pm. This meant that I should be taking the 'fast' bus and not the slow one, but I had no alternative if I was to continue that day. I checked that it ran as a daily service bus, and that I would be paying my fare on the bus – in order to establish that it was not run as a coach with booked tickets. Upon being satisfied about this I boarded the bus and settled down for the long run to Glasgow. Conductor H. King signed my schedule at 3.23pm, even before we moved. The Carlisle to Glasgow 30 single ticket cost 10s 9d. Again I was the only passenger for some time, and I was able to have a chat with Mr King. There was very little traffic on the road, and I kept my map open on my lap, as I was most interested to know when we crossed the border. I think we travelled about 10 miles, then he advised me we were coming to it! We went over a bridge, and then passed near a railway signal box, turned slightly left and we were in Scotland. There seemed very little to get excited about – but I felt that I had reached a goal.

No frontier could have been quieter! No policemen – no barriers of any kind. We just left England behind as if it were of little consequence. I could see no difference so it was some consolation to see a little cottage place marked Gretna Green Forge.

'That's not the real forge, you know!' remarked the conductor, 'Keep your eyes open and look down this turning on the right. See it? It's just down there; you can see the roof, can't you?'

That's the way your dreams go.

My mind came back from its romantic wanderings, and I enquired whether I would be likely to have time to get a cup of tea at a stop on the way. He told me that they stopped for several minutes at Lockerbie, and that there were tearooms nearby where he intended to go himself. That's one of the things I like about bus riding, the conductors and drivers are human too, and have to take a little rest and refreshment occasionally.

At the tearooms at Lockerbie I was thrilled at the sight of Scottish food. At that moment it looked much nicer than ours! I had a wonderful cup of tea, and something nice to eat, and was back on the bus in good time. I sat back in my seat to enjoy Scotland.

This was to be a journey of about four hours and at first there were miles upon miles of lonely roads. I became intrigued with the names over the shops as we came into villages and small towns . . . Macduff . . . MacKay . . . Donald MacDonald . . . MacKenzie. By a bus stop I could count five or six shops on each side within the range of my vision and every one, without exception, had a real Scots sounding name.

The landscape seemed much the same as I had seen earlier – flat and a little uninteresting, but slowly, very slowly I began to notice a change and detect a difference.

I felt so proud to be going to Scotland like this and searching for some vestige of Scottish blood in my veins. My father's name is Andrews – and somehow I wanted to feel that I 'belonged' a little.

After a while I dozed, rocked gently by the motion of the bus. I was feeling comfortably tired after a quiet time in the sunshine. I awoke with a start and bumped my forehead on the side of the window frame.

We had stopped with a jerk behind some traffic – the first I had seen that day. There were shops and business offices, factories and tall tenement flats.

On and on we went with the traffic getting thicker. From the signs on the buses we met we were obviously running into Glasgow. There was some distance still to go to get to the centre of the city, but eventually we pulled round into a bus station.

I'd arrived in Glasgow! It was about 7.30pm. I looked in vain for homespun tartan or some other picturesque evidence of Scotland and had to be content with seeing a boy wearing a tartan beret.

Supper was the first thing to think of just then, so I walked down the street, and turned left, right, left – looking for a pleasant cafe. It wasn't particularly inspiring but when I'm enjoying myself even little things give me a kick and just walking around in Glasgow just then seemed the height of enjoyment. Supper over I walked again and this time I found the Square and the University.

The best part of the city seemed to be near here otherwise I thought it was as noisy as any other city and definitely bigger than I had anticipated. This point made it difficult for me to decide where to look for a small hotel or a guest house and after spending half an hour looking round I thought it would be a good idea to continue the journey if I could get a bus going northward. With this feeling uppermost I made my way back to the bus station and was lucky to hear that I could get on to Stirling that night although I should arrive rather late.

The evening was mild, and the prospect of perhaps another hour on the buses did not worry me at all. There was plenty of life and bustle at the bus station so I took my place in the queue for the bus to Stirling.

By now it was quite dark and there was little to see beyond the occasional headlight of a car. To occupy my time I made a few notes about my journey and studied the map of Scotland to see where my travels would lead to on the 'morrow. I hoped to go up to Perth and on to Pitlochry, Kingussie or Inverness, it was almost impossible to say just how far I could get in a day.

I made a rough estimate too of the distance I had travelled since I had left the Lake District in the morning. It seemed to add up to the amazing total of 175 miles.

The bus I was on from Glasgow to Stirling was the 9.20pm due in at 10.40 and my schedule was signed by a young lady conductor Jenny W. Grant, and as there was an inspector near at hand as we drove into the bus station at Stirling, I asked him for his signature too – to sign me in. This he was kind enough to do for me and I think I was on the last bus, as it was 10.45. (The information was written down by Insp. J. Niven.)

There was plenty of light and movement at the bus depot but going out into the street I felt I had made a mistake in going so far. There were very few people about and it was soon apparent that I should not get into an hotel.

The first one I went into was full up and at the second I could get no reply to a ring at the door. There was only one thing to do, and that was to find a police station. This was not easy as there was no one about to speak to. I felt a little discouraged for a moment – was my enterprise to lose its savour? Was I going to fail now, after going so well?

I thought of going back to the bus station, where there might still be some activity, and on my way there I met a conductor who gave me an address in King Street. This turned out to be a top flat over a shop and I climbed the dark stairs without much feeling of hope.

The lady might have been waiting for me!

'Of course I can put you up! You are very welcome,' was what she said.

I was very relieved and apologised for the lateness of the hour and explained how I had looked round Glasgow, and then come on to Stirling.

We exchanged names, and she showed me into the room. 'But don't go to bed yet, I'd be glad to make you some tea and then I can have a cup myself.' Within a few minutes, I was sitting at the table. There was thinly sliced bread and butter, tomatoes and cheese and home made cake on the table. The teapot was brewing inside a stuffed cosy.

What a welcome! Thank you again Mrs Macgregor!

We sat talking until after midnight. The atmosphere was very friendly and I was very relieved.

'I expect you are tired after such a long journey,' she said. 'You had better go to bed now' – and she began to clear the table.

Oddly enough I did not feel very tired, but it was very late and we had talked for quite a while. I thanked her and went into the bedroom. Probably I should have another long day tomorrow I thought, and was soon fast asleep.

I woke to the sound of lorries and traffic passing and remembered that the room I was in faced the main road. It was barely light, so I got up to look out of the window. The air was fresh and keen like champagne and the sun was showing through a chink in thin clouds. Other clouds were drawn up like curtains to one side as if a hand were lifting them upward from the horizon. Behind the clouds the sky was every conceivable shade of pink and rose. I could not be sure whether this predicted a fine day for me, or not, but it was very beautiful.

Mrs Macgregor offered me a large breakfast but fortunately she mentioned it before she cooked it, because I prefer a light meal. 'Just cereal and some tea, please – or some toast,' I said. After breakfast, she insisted upon packing some ham sandwiches for me – which was very thoughtful of her.

I paid the bill, which was exceedingly modest, and I made a careful note of her address. Whether it is more blessed to give or to accept hospitality, I cannot say, but it is certainly true that some people are born with a gift for making others 'feel at home' – and I felt very much at home in Stirling thanks to my kind hostess in King Street.

Left:
In the summer of 1954 Mrs Leather travelled by bus from London to Lands End and back. This aroused considerable newspaper interest and on her way home she was photographed in St Ives bus station posed on the rear platform of a Western National Bristol. *Daily Sketch*

Right:
The first major stage of the journey from Whitton to John O'Groats was on London Transport service 81 from Hounslow to Slough. An RT is seen here loading in Hounslow. *Ian Allan Collection*

Below:
Reading Corporation trolleybuses were still carrying a substantial proportion of local traffic and this Sunbeam S7 with Park Royal body had by then seen some five years' service. *Don Morris*

Top:
Seen in Gloucester Green bus station at Oxford, Thames Valley 717 was a Bristol LS6B 41-seater with Eastern Coach Works body, one of 16 delivered in 1954-55.
Ian Allan Collection

Above left:
In the 1950s City of Oxford was still taking delivery of lowbridge double-deckers with the upper deck gangway at the side as typified by this AEC Regent III of 1950 with a Park Royal 52-seat body. *A. A. Cooper*

Above:
Another bus seen at Gloucester Green, Oxford, and quite possibly encountered on the next stage of the journey is this Daimler COG5 of Worth's Services, Enstone.
Don Morris

Left:
Relevant as to route number and age of chassis this Leyland Tiger of Stratford Blue seen leaving for Birmingham had been rebodied as a double-decker by Northern Counties in 1963. *M. A. Penn*

Above:
At the time of Mrs Leather's journey the joint Stratford-on-Avon – Birmingham service of Midland Red and Stratford Blue was being maintained so far as the former was concerned by its almost new LD8 double-deckers. *Edward Shirras*

Below:
The Midland Red fleet still contained a mixture of pre- and postwar buses and this view at Coventry bus station includes a Brush-bodied SON single-decker of 1939 and one of the 100 AEC Regents delivered in 1946. This one had a Metro-Cammell body. *T. W. Moore*

Above:
Almost the last of the forward-entrance double-deckers with normal front engine position was Midland Red 2377, one of 50 FEDD type built in 1939 and here seen in Edmund Street, Birmingham, some 16 years later. *Don Morris*

Left:
A Brush-bodied Leyland Titan PD2 followed by a Crossley-bodied Daimler CVG6 of Birmingham City Transport climb Hill Street, Birmingham. *T. W. Moore*

Below left:
Park Royal bodywork was used by Birmingham relatively infrequently but it was fitted to 15 AEC Regent IIIs in 1947 (seen here) and to 50 Leyland Titan PD2s in 1949-50. *T. W. Moore*

Top right:
Rounding the Council House in Birmingham is one of 270 Crossley double-deckers with Crossley bodywork delivered in 1949-50. *T. W. Moore*

Centre right:
No more Crossley chassis were ordered but Crossley bodywork was again supplied in 1952 and then in 1953-54 when two batches of 125 on Daimler CVG6 chassis were supplied. 2812, seen by Birmingham Council House, was one of the earlier batch. *T. W. Moore*

Right:
The activities of what was then Burton-on-Trent Corporation were more confined than those of the East Staffordshire undertaking. Double-deck operation began only in 1944 and this Guy Arab III of 1947 was one of six with Roberts lowbridge bodies. *T. W. Moore*

Right:
In common with a considerable number of operators Burton took advantage of the availability secondhand of ex-London Transport utility double-deckers. This Guy Arab had Park Royal bodywork.   *T. W. Moore Collection*

Below:
In 1952 Barton Transport rebuilt a prewar Leyland Tiger chassis for dual-purpose operation and it is seen here at Derby a year or so later.   *Don Morris*

Bottom:
Felix Bus Service of Stanley operated this Dennis Lancet for 21 years. It entered service in 1935 with a Willowbrook body which was rebuilt by Yeates in 1947 when it was given a diesel engine. It is seen in Derby bus station.   *Don Morris*

Above:
A Sunbeam F4 trolleybus of Derby Corporation Transport with Brush bodywork is seen in Derby marketplace. *T. W. Moore*

Right:
Also seen in the marketplace is one of five Crossley DD42/8As built in 1952. *T. W. Moore*

Below:
The route from Derby was via Matlock to Buxton and was made in fact on a North Western journey on the joint service with Trent. Until Cromford, however, the territory was more that of the latter company and so it is not inappropriate to include this picture of an AEC Regal II with Willowbrook bodywork dating from 1946. *T. W. Moore*

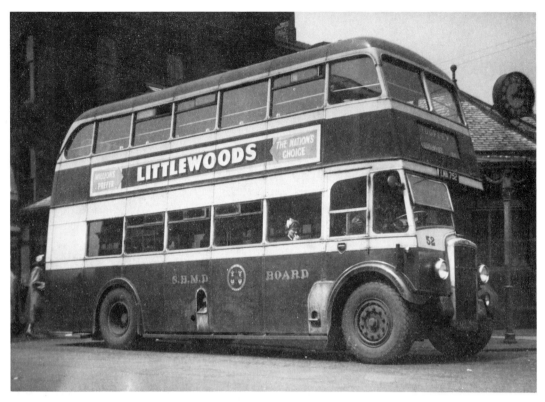

Above:
Buxton to Manchester was another North Western ride albeit in warmth-induced drowsiness and the bus was approaching the centre of Manchester by the time Mrs Leather had awakened. To be seen to the south-west of the city were the Daimlers of the Stalybridge, Hyde, Mossley and Dukinfield Transport & Electricity Board more usually referred to as the SHMD. This CVD6 entered service with an East Lancashire body in 1949. *Don Morris*

Above left:
Entering Piccadilly, Manchester, in 1955 is North Western Bristol K5G 452 which had entered service in 1939 and been rebodied by Willowbrook a dozen years later. *Don Morris*

Left:
Manchester's last batch of trolleybuses – Burlingham-bodied BUT9612Ts – would just have entered service when Mrs Leather's trip took place. *Don Morris*

Below left:
Some six years earlier a view of Piccadilly bus station includes a Brush-bodied Daimler CVG5, a Crossley and a prewar Leyland Titan of Manchester together with a North Western Bristol K5G. *Alan Cooper*

Above right:
Mrs Leather's main interest in Salford was a fire but more than 100 of the Metro-Cammell-bodied Daimler CVG6s had been delivered to Salford City Transport in 1952 and were to be seen in many places. *Don Morris*

Right:
One of the Leyland-bodied Leyland Titan PD2/12s delivered to Ribble in 1952 is seen in Bolton Moor Street bus station en route for Blackpool. *G. H. F. Atkins*

Top left:
In the bus station at Lancaster is Lancaster City Transport 70; a Daimler CWG5 dating back to 1943 with a Crossley body built in 1952. *C. B. Golding*

Top right:
Another of the vehicles in the bus station was one of the Ribble Leyland Titan TD5s dating from 1938 which had been rebodied by Eastern Coach Works in 1948. *Edward Shirras*

Above:
Also in Lancaster bus station in the summer of 1955 is Ribble 211, a Leyland Tiger TS7 of 1935 with a 1949 Burlingham body. Behind is, 424, a Saro-bodied Leyland Tiger Cub. *A. M. Wright*

Left:
By 1955 the original Ribble White Ladies with fully-fronted Burlingham coach bodies on Leyland Titan PD1/3 chassis were being repainted in bus livery as exemplified by 1222. *A. M. Wright*

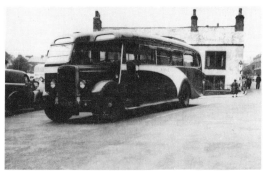

Above:
The once numerous Leyland Cheetahs in the Ribble fleet were becoming few and far between but this one, converted to oil, is seen in Ambleside bus station.
Edward Shirras

Left:
Seen actually in Penrith these Leyland Tiger TS8s dating from 1939-40 were by now engaged mostly on bus work. The body of 1167 was by Duple. *Edward Shirras*

Below:
The journey from Keswick to Carlisle was on a Cumberland bus. This Massey-bodied Leyland Titan TD4 is, however, seen in Cockermouth. *R. C. Davis*

Above:
Loading outside Carlisle station is Ribble 377, an all-Leyland Royal Tiger on an outward journey to Goose Green.
Edward Shirras

Left:
Also outside the station is Ribble 292, a Sentinel-Beadle then operated in the Carlisle area. *Edward Shirras*

Below:
Failure to connect with the Western SMT bus to Glasgow at Carlisle was offset by the ability to catch the Ribble X30 13min later which gave a Glasgow arrival some 70min earlier. Rebodied in 1949 by Duple Ribble Leyland Tiger TS8 729 was still working on limited stop as well as bus services. *Ian Allan Collection*

Above:
Alexander buses for the north left Glasgow from either Buchanan Street or Dundas Street. A typical scene shows the now-demolished houses of Parliamentary Road with WG 9492 (P656) entering Dundas Street bus station. This was an Alexander-bodied Leyland Tiger TS8 new in 1940. *Robert Grieves*

Left:
New Alexander vehicles in 1954 had included AC11 with Park Royal bodywork on an AEC Reliance chassis. It was one of a growing number of this type. *J. Thomson*

Below:
The original Gretna Green Old Blacksmith's Shop at the Headlesscross where thousands of weddings took place 'over the anvil' prior to 1940. *Scottish Tourist Board*

Chapter 6

'I'd like to wish you a very happy journey,' said Mrs Macgregor, as I left her. 'It has been a very exciting experience for *me* – meeting you!' Now wasn't that nice of her – when I was the one who was indebted to her. I had had a peep into her life and she into mine, and it was obvious that we had both enjoyed the encounter.

There was time for a saunter round Stirling before going to the bus depot, so I made my way along the main road and in a few minutes I was captivated by the shops – especially the food shops. They were a sight to see! Scottish beef and hams, joints that looked quite twice as large as those I see when I go shopping, lay behind the plate glass windows.

The buns and scones, fancy bread and shortbread were almost bursting out of the baker's shop windows. Of course, it was early yet; barely half past eight and the shoppers had not yet begun to buy. Fruit and vegetables – all looking extremely fresh and inviting, lay in attractive piles or in baskets.

I passed slowly by and on to the bus, but first I had to make enquiries. I expected to be able to go to Perth, Dunkeld, Pitlochry, Blair Atholl, Kingussie, Aviemore, etc, in short hops and so through to the town of Inverness.

'Yes, you can go that way but the only means of travelling that route from here is by long distance bus and in that case you will not have to change at all,' said the girl at the counter in the enquiry office.

'Is there any other way?' I asked.

'No, not if you want to go to Inverness,' was the reply. So long as it was a daily service bus, picking up at regular bus stops all the way and I could pay the conductor for my ticket (and not have to 'book') I was satisfied that it was a *bus*, and not a *coach*. How far it went, did not matter to me at all; the further – in this case along my path – the better.

The bus came into the bus station, and I was most impressed but vaguely worried. It was all too comfortable for my liking. I had expected a hard seat, and here was I being offered a well-upholstered seat and a foot rest! It only needed a sun blind to make it perfect, for the sun came out and I was baked. I put on my sun glasses and rolled up the sleeves of my blouse, and sank down in the seat.

To salve my conscience I asked an official to put a note on my schedule which he obligingly did.

It reads,

Stirling bus station . . . 9.30 a.m.
Inspector A. Norton.
The only means of travelling from here is by long distance bus.
Conductor's signature and the fare.
G. McLeod.
Stirling to Inverness 16/9.

I added the ticket to the others in a rubber band, and settled down to a record run.

For a while my eyes were glued to the windows as we pulled slowly out of Stirling then down went the driver's accelerator just after leaving the cross roads – and away we went.

The miles disappeared under the wheels as we took to the open road. I felt as though I was on a yacht. I had never heard of most of the places that we passed. This was motoring as a tourist not the type of bus riding I had been used to. But who was I to grumble – instead I was delighted with the change.

We ran into a marketplace and the bus filled up, and I found myself with a seat companion. Almost at once we were chatting together and getting acquainted. I could not have had a brighter companion. Her charm was wholly independent of the fact that she was Australian although I spotted the fact the moment she spoke to me. She wore a white blouse and a tweed skirt, and carried a brown calf shoulder bag very much like the one I had myself. She was fair and very tanned and she was obviously very interested in the journey that we were taking. She told me that she had saved for four years to come here on holiday and she was on her way to Strathpeffer where she would be staying at a hostel. We found the place together on the map, thereby learning that we would both be going the full distance on the bus, through to Inverness.

Strathpeffer was a little to the northwest of Inverness while my subsequent journey would carry me on up the east coast of Scotland. We chatted our way through Perth and Bankfoot.

The wide curving stretches of road gave way to a climb as we approached Dunkeld. Now there were mountains on both sides with the River Tay curving gently to the left of the road. We felt the solitude and silence of the Highlands and enjoyed the scene of loch and forest as we passed. In the course of our conversation she had glanced once or twice at a man who was sitting opposite her across the centre gangway. He was a youngish man with a small moustache and I noticed that he had a pipe in his hand and a tobacco pouch on his knee.

'I love the smell of tobacco!' she whispered to me.

I smiled agreement and we both waited for him to light up.

It was about 12 miles from Dunkeld to Pitlochry through magnificent scenery and we had just left Dunkeld when she made the remark. The River Tay disappeared off to the left and another, smaller, river took its place. We stopped at Pitlochry and then went through the Pass of Killiecrankie and still he did not light up. He polished the pipe on his handkerchief and smoothed it down his nose. He filled it with tobacco pressing the little brown flakes down with his thumb, but still he did not light up.

The mountains, crags and trees closed in around us, and we stopped at Blair Atholl but still the pipe remained unlit. Thirty miles of glen and forest kept all eyes to the windows and when we glanced at him again, over an hour later the tobacco pouch had been put away, and the pipe remained cold in his hand.

He had forgotten it entirely!

The conductor pointed out places to us where there should have been waterfalls but we saw only the merest trickle of water and the river itself had petered out to a little stream playing over the boulders that made the river bed. The dry hot summer had taken its toll, and now there was a drought.

Tree trunks lying against the banks were even being bleached white by the scorching sunshine.

The incident of the forgotten pipe amused us both but it also proved how absorbing the scenery was. Later, at Kingussie we pulled on to a wide gravel path that had been made between the fir trees outside a tea room and came to a stop. The conductor told us that we would not be leaving for about 20 minutes, and that there would be time to get some tea.

The Australian girl and I went into the tearoom together and gave an order. In a couple of minutes we were joined by the young gentleman with the moustache, and as there was no other seat available, he sat at our table. We had tea and scones and butter . . . then out came the pipe again.

'Do you mind if I smoke?' he said. And then with the frankness that is typical of all Colonials, my companion laughed and told him that she had been waiting for him to do so for the past two hours. He looked so mystified that I began to giggle helplessly. I felt embarrassed for the gentleman, but between us, we managed to explain and all was well. He lit up and left the tearoom.

Outside a solitary piper was marching up and down, vigorously playing the bagpipes and collecting pennies from the other passengers. We supported him generously with our voluntary contributions from the open doorway of the bus. The sound of the bagpipes mingled with the smell of the blended tobacco and the lovely scenery as we moved out of Kingussie.

Soon we were speeding along the road again amid superb scenery. The misty grey mountain peaks that were in the distance appeared to part to make way for us as we came to them, and the pine trees and lochs fell away behind us. Sometimes we were travelling close to the waters' edge with only a few pink and grey granite rocks between us and the edge of the loch – at others we would be cruising through flat mountain passes that were bare of trees and vegetation.

Sometimes we could see ahead patches of snow lying in the hollows of the crest – and on one occasion we saw snow on the top of a mountain and a fire caused by the sun on rough grass on lower slopes. The smoke intermingled with the purple of the heather and the blue-green shades of the little christmas trees as it lifted.

Reflections in the water as we passed were another attraction. Often the water level was very low – a calm mirror rippled slowly over a sandy bed. When this was the case the reflections were thin and light – but when there was plenty of water in the loch, we had a double picture of mountains, trees and crags as we drifted past. And the reflection was rich and colourful, almost prettier than the view that made it.

Valley succeeded valley in a never-ending display. When you descended there would be a little cluster of cottages, perhaps a shop or two and a creeper or ivy-clad church in the centre of the village.

Presently we arrived at Aviemore for another pause amid silver birch trees. I was told that it is possible to ski here in the winter, for it is the winter resort of the Central Highlands.

My Australian companion and I had been overawed by the magnificent scenery, and had scarcely said a word, but she did tell me that she was achieving an almost undreamed of ambition to see the Highlands.

That went for me too!

One perfect picture after another of lochs framed in branches of pine and jewels of mountain scenery left us almost speechless.

We had left Stirling at 9.30am and were due in at Inverness at 5.37pm so the journey took about eight hours.

There had been several pauses on the way and we arrived feeling good for another two hours travelling at least.

My companion was going on to Strathpeffer during the evening, so I decided to continue the journey until dark. We waved each other goodbye.

Chapter 7

My decision to continue further that evening meant that I would probably reach Invergordon, so I made enquiries at the Highland Omnibus office in the Station Square at Inverness, and had my schedule signed by Miss Kay Barron who gave me the information I wanted to know. A bus for Invergordon would leave at seven o'clock, I was told, so as it was about six, I had an hour for refreshment before leaving.

I had a hot meal and looked at one or two shops before making my way to the bus.

At 6.50pm I boarded the bus for that part of the journey which was probably the most exciting of all – the road to the distant north. Few people I know have been so far. I was being urged on by the powerful feeling of anticipation, and I would not stop while I could go on . . . and on!

At Inverness the road bends off to the west for about 14 miles around Beauly Firth before turning north for Beauly and Muir of Ord. The road runs near the sea for most of the way with a line of fishing villages for the herring fleet.

The distance would be about 40 miles between the town of Inverness and Invergordon because of the encroachment of the North Sea, with a fertile plain of the Black Isle between.

The scenery here had changed, but was still very interesting. Now it was quieter with homely whitewashed little cottages and small farm houses.

The fare was 3s 5d single, and my pencilled schedule was signed by Miss Joan Munro. We travelled the road to Invergordon as if on the crest of a land-wave, sometimes I found myself peering down at the sea over the edge of a rugged cliff while at other times we were just skimming along a lonely road that dipped and swayed between lowland farms. The bus pulled up outside the railway station at Dingwall and I got down from the bus to stretch my legs when I saw that both the conductor and the driver had disappeared into a small office beside the entrance to the station.

I was attracted to a tall wooden cross, set high on a square of grass. Keeping half an eye on the driver's seat I walked over to it. It stood tall and proud although the cross arms were pathetically askew. There was an inscription in French on it with a date . . . 1917.

I went back to the bus and spoke to a gentleman sitting inside, telling him that I was outside by the green and would he kindly warn me if the conductor came back and I did not. I told him I wanted to copy the inscription on the cross.

'Its the original cross to the 4th Battalion Seaforth Highlanders that was set up in France after the battle of Cambrai,' he told me. I thanked him and went back to make a correct copy of the inscription, which reads as follows.

Mort pour la Patrie
4 eme Bataillon
Les Seaforth Highlanders
Honneur aux Hommes
Mobilises dans cet village
Pour la Bataille de Cambrai 1917.

Perhaps it was the slim tallness of it, or may have been because it was the original memorial – I though it was the most touching thing I have ever seen.

As I moved away, the driver and conductor reappeared – or it may have been two other people . . . I had very quickly to resume my seat on top of the bus.

'You'd be a stranger here, I think,' ventured a woman nearby as I sat down again.

'Yes, I come from London,' I told her.

'Did ye never coom this way before?'

'No, I'd never even been to Scotland until this week.'

'And ye coom from London!' she repeated.

And when I explained that I had not only come from London, but had come all the way by buses, she turned to a man with her 'Did ye ever hear the like o' that?'

'We knew ye must be a stranger,' said another, 'we know those words by heart.' Then she quoted the rest of the information that I had seen but not written down. It went, 'This cross was brought home from France in 1924, and re-erected by the 4th Seaforth Reunion Club 1914 – 1918 in memory of their beloved dead.'

'No burdens yonder – all sorrows past.

No burdens yonder – home at last.'

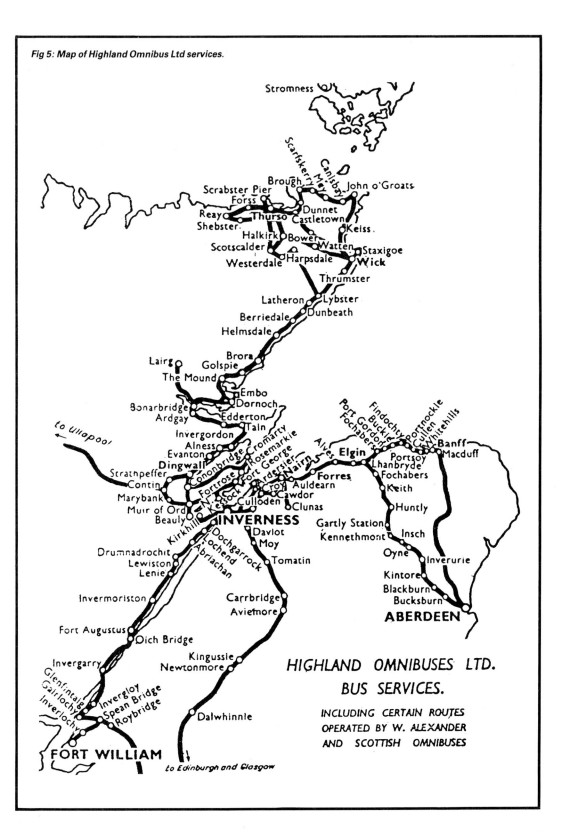

Fig 5: Map of Highland Omnibus Ltd services.

HIGHLAND OMNIBUSES LTD.
BUS SERVICES.

INCLUDING CERTAIN ROUTES
OPERATED BY W. ALEXANDER
AND SCOTTISH OMNIBUSES

The bus had left Dingwall station yard and was now travelling on a road which bordered the North Sea. We talked for a while and I had their company for about six miles, and they left the bus at Evanton. We continued beside the water of Cromarty Firth through Alness and on to Invergordon.

The bus pulled up in the High Street of Invergordon and my travels were over for the day. There were groups of young naval cadets in the street, and a few in the cafe where I enquired about accommodation.

'Just across the road you will find Mrs MacKenzie,' I was told and I did not have to go any further. I was made very welcome and shown to a front bedroom. Looking out of the window over the rooftops of the houses opposite I could see a white boat on a blue-grey strip of sea. Gazing immediately below there were several Naval boys turning down the road opposite the house. My eyes became accustomed to the distance, and the little white boats which at first looked like little toys became slim ships in the harbour. They may have been destroyers, but I did not know and did not like to ask.

Supper and a comfortable room with breakfast before I left again in the morning. Only a small bill to pay and a few sandwiches in my bag for the journey. A pleasant smile and a word to cheer me on the way from Mrs MacKenzie.

A brilliant sun was shining the full length of the road as I left her house in the morning for my final day of bus riding in that direction.

I hoped to be in John O'Groats by nightfall. Mustn't forget to call at Wick Post Office!

Chapter 8

I had had beautiful sunshine all the way, and now I was on the 'last leg' of the journey. It was Wednesday and I had been travelling since Friday. The bus left from just outside Mrs MacKenzie's house in the High Street at 8.46am and the road nearly all the way lies close to the sea. At first this would be Cromarty Bay and Nigg Bay but later it was Dornoch Firth and then the broad expanse of the North Sea. This coastline was on my right, so sitting on the right hand side of the bus, I had the sea for company all the way.

I love the beginning of a journey especially if it is early in the morning. There is a special quality of excitement and anticipation about it – and today I was really travelling the road far north. This last day's bus journey from Invergordon to John O'Groats covered two whole pages in my daughter's school atlas and it was from this that I could see that the main road sweeps up along the coast the whole way. From this too, I read the names of all the little bays and points that make up this unusual stretch of country.

What the map did not show, and what you would not expect is that because of the nearness of the mountains to the sea you get some of the most magnificent scenery you could imagine.

As we went along the air became colder and the aspect bleaker but it still remained, for me, a golden day.

The heather too, looked amazing as it stretched away before me over the hills. There were literally miles of it. I hoped that I could get some to take home. The road ran across to Tain and backed inland for about 10 miles. You could see the road opposite, way over on the other side of Dornoch Firth. It looked quite close but the conductor told me that it would be an hour before we reached it. We turned the hairpin bend at Bonar Bridge with the Kyle of Sutherland and Oykell River going inland. We swung off again for another 10 miles before reaching Dornoch itself.

I was told that motorists usually miss this wonderful old town, because it lies a few miles east of the main road. But the bus went into Dornoch and I went with it.

I became completely absorbed in the view of a ruin that stood in a little bay close to the sea. We saw it as we approached from the south, and again from the west, and finally from the north for this corkscrew of a road practically turned a somersault round it. I am not sure but I think it was the ruin of an old mill called Spinningdale Cotton Mill. The bus might have been on skates the way we coasted up and up, then down and down again.

Often the road was so deserted that I thought we had left civilisation behind for sure, but in a short while we would coast down a hill again and into a valley. There would be a river ahead and a cluster of cottages that denoted another village.

Skibo Castle was pointed out to me as being the home of the late Mr Andrew Carnegie. Please excuse me if I am wrong but the story runs that there are 365 windows with a different view for each day of the year, and I could easily believe it for each turret and gable appeared to turn in a different direction and the windows looked like faces with eyes and open doors for nose and mouths. Below the castle there were sunken lawns and flower gardens.

We reached Dornoch at 10.50am and my schedule which by now covered four pages of card was signed by Jen MacKay 151. It was on this bus that I met Inspector Grant.

'All this beautiful heather!' I said, 'and I can't get out and pick one piece. I certainly hoped to get a bit of heather to take back to London with me.'

'Oh, I'll see you get some heather,' he promised. 'When will you be coming back this way?'

We worked it out together. He reckoned it was about 158 miles from Inverness to John O'Groats and that I still had about 86 miles to go, to get to the turning point of my journey.

'I'll gather it for you and leave it at the office in Dingwall – you'll be back there sometime tomorrow,' he said.

' . . . or the day after!' was my reply.

The end of the journey still seemed remote, and to get back to Dingwall which I had come through during the afternoon of yesterday, I should have to travel another 86 miles to John O'Groats plus the 86 miles back to where we were then, as well as the 26 miles back to Dingwall. A distance of about 198 miles!

I thanked him and made a note about it on my schedule or I felt I should forget where he had told me to call for it.

We passed Loch Fleet with the Strath flowing away to the west and on into Golspie. Then I saw Dunrobin Castle and the road smoothed itself out as we ran into Brora.

Now I knew something about Brora. Among my hobbies I have made handwoven tweed. It would be made from roughly twisted wool and as the shuttle moved from one side of the loom to another, little knobbly bits would stick out giving the material a very rough hairy surface that was not very professional looking. Sometimes I would wash, shrink and press it myself – then I was told to send it to Brora.

Off to Brora it went, a bulky parcel in the post. And back it came, the cloth was smooth to the touch with every thread in its place. The bumps were gone and it had been properly shrunk, pressed and neatly rolled up.

There was no need to ask where the tweed mills were, the chimneys could be seen from far off, and I leaned out of the window to get a closer look at the factory where my tweed had been professionally 'finished'.

I was also naturally interested to see a shop full of lovely heathery looking tweed materials in the window as we stopped at the parking spot in Brora. I got out of the bus as soon as the lady conductor had disappeared – to have a closer look at the window display and to see the cloth in its native surroundings.

It may have been a small thing but I was very thrilled to have the opportunity of seeing Brora at close quarters.

I returned to the bus as the lady conductor reappeared. She had brought me a wee piece of white heather! 'For luck,' she said as she gave it to me.

Wasn't that kind of her? I pinned it to my coat and wore it for the rest of the journey. Thank you again Miss MacKay.

We were back on the open road for the 12 miles into Helmsdale. Somewhere along this road the bus crews changed over and Inspector Grant and Miss MacKay left me.

Miss C. W. Davison took the lady conductor's place and I chatted with her for a while. There were no other passengers for miles and miles.

'I read about your trip,' she told me, 'and I wondered whether you might be on my bus!'

'I am proud to be on your bus,' was my reply – and so I was. These buses had opened up the country to me and I was grateful. I was more than grateful – I was enthusiastic about the buses, and out to prove that a person like me could go thousands of miles on ordinary buses and have both an education and a holiday at the same time. I told her so, too. We chatted our way over the hills to Helmsdale, another 12 miles of the road by the sea. I took a return ticket for this part of the journey

as I would be returning the same way. The cost was 13s 6d and it was duly placed with the others in the rubber band.

The Highland bus drew into Helmsdale and over the bridge to pull up in the narrow street at 12.15. I said farewell to the lady conductor who told me where I would find the bus stop, for my next bus – to Wick – which was not until 3.15pm. I had three hours to wait. Sounds a bit grim, doesn't it? Well it meant that I had time for a good meal, if I could find one. I retraced my steps to the bridge where I saw a hotel, and wandered in. It was a grey stone building, and not particularly imposing from the outside. There was a small panelled lobby, leading through to a corridor and another door near at hand on the left. I chose this door and found myself in an empty bar. I walked over to the windows which were hung with heavy tartan material – and hand-woven – a gay plaid with bright red in it.

A voice behind me said, 'I'm sorry but this bar is closed.'

'I was attracted to your curtains. All that lovely material. There must be twenty yards of it there. What tartan is it?'

'The Royal Stewart!' came the reply.

It looked so warm and hung in beautiful folds and being hand-woven it would last for ever.

I was gently directed to the dining room, which was the other way down the corridor and found myself in a lofty room decorated with stag antlers and hunting pictures.

Steak and kidney pie – a very generous portion with vegetables, redcurrant tart and cream, and a cup of coffee sounded very nice, and turned out to be delicious. I made up for one or two meals I had missed! The cost was 5s 6d, and I lingered over it for about an hour – chatting for a few minutes with a young man sitting at a table, working on some accounts.

When I thought I could not very well stay there any longer I found the ladies toilet room for a wash and brush up and left the hotel to seek another diversion. I walked to the bridge and found a spot where I could get down to the river, over the rough grass.

I sat down for a while in the sunshine resting my back against a fallen tree. The shadow of a small fern growing beneath the bark waved gently in the breeze. Around me the grass was russet brown and green in the sun. It was a delightful spot for a laze. A few scrub trees were growing here and there, but otherwise the slope was bare down to the water's edge.

Over on the other side the hills shut out half the skyline and came down to meet the river as it disappeared in the west. An old boat had been pulled up on the bank, and it lay over on its side – a forgotten thing, probably rotting with age, but too far away from me to see the holes in its side. The bed of the river was visible under the water and formed banks of rocks on both sides, some worn smooth with the movement of the water, others sticking up pink, grey and black according to whether they were in the sun or not.

Something stirred in the grass at my elbow and for a second I saw a bird eyeing me with disapproval. I tried to keep still but in a moment or two I had stirred a little and the bark of the tree snapped behind me and the bird took to its wings and flew away.

I got up and walked in the shade, down by the rocks watching the lazy river lapping against the wall of the harbour. There did not seem time enough to go far away. Supposing I missed the bus! It was much too important to me and I was content to wander near the bridge and the bus stop, not going far in any direction.

Finally it came! I was standing by the road sign which read 'To Wick' and I asked a passerby if she would kindly take a snapshot of me standing there. It would be a memento of my patience. It was a Highland omnibus, and it waited by the bus stop for another 15 minutes before leaving.

My schedule reads, 'Left Helmsdale 3.15pm for Wick. Conductor Janetta Sutherland . . . fare 9s 6d return.'

We ran through a narrow street or two, and out into the country of the hills. In a few minutes I could look back on Helmsdale harbour with the River Helmsdale flowing off to the northwest. The road twisted and turned and Helmsdale was immediately lost and the slopes of Creag on Oirdiriah took its place.

Below on the coastal side lay the Ord of Caithness. We travelled across the bleak face of many heights and skimmed along the edge of bracken moors. Inland a bit and the sea disappeared from view, but not for long, another twist and turn and there it was again, silver grey and greeny blue in the afternoon sunshine. Hill followed hill in a never ending procession and then a magnificent view of trees and glens. The road became dark with trees and we turned the bend of Berridale, surely one of the most attractive spots nature ever designed. Another corkscrew turn and we began to climb again, passing a whitewashed forge covered with stags' antlers; for a few minutes they looked like dozens of hat racks sticking out from the walls and then we came closer and the pattern of 'V' shapes became single antlers as the driver pulled round the bend and close to the old smithy.

The lady conductor told me that Berriedale Hill was almost impassable during the winter when the snow filled the valley and hid the curves of the road, but today the trees were green and it was utterly delightful to see such magnificent views and to coast round the bends in the road.

We stopped at Berriedale at about 4pm. Beyond us to the left was Langwell Forest and ahead another 10 miles of coastal road. I was told the bus made this journey three times a day during the week but from Dunbeath a few miles to the north the bus was more frequent with seven or eight buses that went through to Wick. On Sundays there were two buses that did the full journey from Helmsdale to Wick, with an extra bus from Berriedale.

At Dunbeath we left the mountains behind, and the country became flat and open. We crossed several rivers on the way to Latheron and Lybster. At every turn there was a creek or a bay. You could see for miles – a flat treeless country with the road stretching away ahead.

This was Caithness, the last county on the map, and I found the journey fascinating. Here and there you could see a whitewashed cottage cuddled into the landscape, and as the bus pulled up at a bus stop I caught a glimpse of honeysuckle in a garden. It seemed a strange place to find honeysuckle but I noticed it several times. The gardens were tiny, just a few feet square and enclosed by walls to keep out the wind . . . and how the wind must blow in from the sea and the mist gather on the mainland.

A low rock wall edged the road and the crevices in some places were filled in with earth and little tufts of grass grew out to add to the rugged look.

Curiosity made me look closely into the doorways of these Highland homes. The windows were small and the walls were very thick and a heavy thatch made the roof. I wondered what they would be like inside. Anyone there would be able to see the bus coming for miles, and as we came up to a cottage often someone would appear in the doorway and join the bus. The driver pulled up several times; there seemed to be no special bus stops and if there were, they were not marked in any way. We took aboard passengers and parcels alike and the space up near the driver was piled high with boxes.

We would draw up near a cottage – 'It's a box for Wullee,' was the shout as someone appeared at the open door.

'Aw reet,' came the answer, and the box would be swung off the open door and come to rest on the grass by the gate . . . and William of the little Highland homestead would get his parcel.

And the bus went on and on.

We got to Wick at about five o'clock. It had taken us two hours and I was told that the distance was about 38 miles. The bus pulled into the town, over a bridge and stopped near the shops.

Now for the Post Office to see if anyone had sent me a letter for I had given my address as Care of the Post Office at Wick, as it was the nearest town to John O'Groats. I had only another 18 miles to go to keep my promise . . . to journey to John O'Groats by bus.

I walked round to the right in the main road and found the Post Office.

'So you're Mrs Leather! We wondered when you might arrive,' was the reply to my question and I was handed a bunch of letters and cards.

There were 16 postcards, three letters and the registered letter with the pennant flag in it, plus 20 cigarettes and a pound note which I had posted to myself as a 'prize' for doing the journey. I would save this to open at the end of the journey. The girls at the counter were very interested.

How nice of so many people to write. The cards were from friends, wishing me luck or congratulating me on my enterprise and I was very thrilled to have them. The letters were from the family and full of general news.

I went into a cafe for some tea and sat down to read. The postcards were of places near my home. There was a picture of the Pagoda at Kew Gardens, another of Hampton Court, one of the Strand on the Green at Chiswick, even one of our local High Street with its shops and Post Office – all with messages to wish me luck and hoping that I had arrived without incidents of misfortune.

My home seemed *very* far away, and yet I might quite truthfully say that I felt at home all the time, a bewildering thought.

Tea over, I found a shop which sold postcards with local views on them. I must let my friends know that I had arrived and what sort of place it was that I had come to. Finally I returned to the Post Office to get some stamps.

There was time for a chat with the lady at the counter who had greeted me on my arrival. I showed her my schedule and bundle of bus tickets and she was very interested. I though it would be nice to have her signature too – that I arrived at Wick, so she signed it 'L.A. MacDonald. P & T.O.P.O. WICK.'

The bus for John O'Groats was due out at 6.5pm and you can bet that I was in my seat in good time. The very last bus for the outward journey.

The skyline of Wick with rooftops and chimneys was soon behind me and we were out on the open road again. It was a beautiful evening and my spirits were riding high. In a short while I would have achieved my ambition – to get to the northerly tip of Scotland by ordinary buses; and I could begin to make plans for the return journey.

But first I hoped to see the Queen Mother's Castle – the Castle of Mey. It lay over to the west a few miles. My schedule was signed by Miss S. Manson (161) and I pocketed ticket No Nq 7704 which cost me 2s single and peered hard ahead, waiting to get my first glimpse of the promised goal.

A long straight road lay ahead as far as the eye could see. Here and there were whitewashed cottages, which I must call 'crofts', with thatched roofs and a small chimney or so. A few sheep were scattered over the distance – lazily munching at the grass. The air was clear and gave promise of a glorious evening but how can I describe the loneliness of it? There was not a tree in sight and the heather had given way to short rough grass. In the hollows lay the peat bogs. I began to recognise these drifts of darker grass among the yellow green of the ordinary landscape. Miss Manson pointed them out to me at first and then I could tell the difference myself.

From Wick to Keiss we had several passengers and again the front was piled high with boxes and cartons.

This was no time to keep 'mysel-to-mysel', and I talked to anyone who would listen. They all seemed to know each other despite the fact that many of them lived miles from the others.

Soon they knew who I was and where I had come from. They were particularly interested in the postcards that I had received from home and these were passed round the bus. In a few minutes we were all chatting together, and they asked me about Buckingham Palace and Trafalgar Square, and one of them asked me whether I knew Fulham. She had a relative who lived there, so I told her all I could about Fulham, and Chelsea and the surrounding neighbourhood.

Suddenly we found ourselves in Keiss, and there was a general exodus, with much collection of luggage and boxes and a lifting about of heavy shopping baskets.

'Gud luck to ye,' said one.

'Ay, ay,' said another.

'If ye no get a bed tonight, ye'll be welcome at me hame here,' said another Scotswoman.

'But I don't know where you live!' I said quickly, anxious not to miss such a generous offer.

'See the hoos wi the red roof. That's where ye'll find me,' she shouted. The bus was already on the move, so I stood on the step and waved my thanks.

'What place is that?' I asked Miss Manson, the lady conductor.

'Keiss,' she told me, 'and you've about nine miles to go now.'

I was the only passenger left on the bus, and although we stopped several times to throw off a parcel at a little home no-one else got on the bus.

'What time will we arrive?' I asked.

'We get in about 7 o'clock. The hotel will be waiting for their ice-cream for dinner,' she said, indicating a large carton among the remaining packages. 'Come and sit up front and meet Mr Mowatt,' Miss Manson suggested.

So I sat up front and we talked together – the driver, the conductor and the passenger to John O'Groats.

We were passing some ruined homesteads. The whitewash had flaked off and the thatch roof had fallen in, and the little place had an air of dejection about it. Sheep nibbled at the grass which had grown inside the open doorway. I remarked that it seemed a bit of a shame feeling that the owner had moved away to better surroundings because he could not make a living.

'You can save your sympathy! The people just build themselves another house nearby,' was the reply.

'Why do they leave them like that, then?' It seemed an obvious question. I could see no good reason for leaving the ruins to fall down by themselves.

'They make shelter for the sheep in the winter.'

Bit by bit I was learning. Here was a reason for the unreasonable, and I could visualise the sheep getting a little protection from the wind and snow, huddling inside the stone walls of the broken down homes. Later, I noticed that in some cases the new home had been built right on to the ruined one, with the end wall serving for both.

There were pretty sights too. Looking towards the sea, on one occasion I saw a little cottage with a garden bigger than the rest. The end facing the road was trimly covered with an evergreen, cut to the shape of a heart. It looked charming on the whitewashed surface. Again and again I caught sight of honeysuckle blooming among the few gardens bushes. The road twisted inland a little and lost sight of the sea but the land was as flat as it was before but with trim little fields and sandy roads here and there. In the far distance, I could see two or three houses, which I was told was the village of John O'Groats.

We were coming into it at last.

The bus turned off to a wide road on the left, and in a few minutes we drew up alongside the open door of John O'Groats hotel.

I had arrived! It was 7pm exactly.

The lady conductor disappeared with the carton of ice-cream and the driver, Mr William J. Mowatt, signed my schedule with the important words.

Arrived John O'Groats Hotel, 7pm
27th July 1955
(C24 bus) William J. Mowatt
'Broo'
John O'Groats
Wick, Scotland

I chatted for a while with Mr Mowatt and asked him if there was a bus to the Queen Mother's Castle – the Castle of Mey.

No, there was no bus, but if I would wait while he changed his coat, he would be pleased to run me over there in his car. He also enquired at the hotel about a room for me for the night and came back to tell me that it was absolutely full up. I wandered into the hotel just to look round and saw the waves beating up against the cliffs under its very walls.

The building stood on the edge of the world, so far as I could see. There was a flagstaff which I was told was erected on the original site of John O'Groats house. There were a few cars parked up on the windswept grass.

Inside the hotel the atmosphere was friendly and Mr Mowatt introduced me to a Scottish newspaper reporter who said he was interested to hear about my journey. We were joined in the bar with a small group of people and all chatted together over a drink to celebrate the occasion for me.

'Don't worry about a room for the night, I'll find you one somewhere.' said my friendly driver as we came out again.

Mr Mowatt took my photograph on the steps of the bus and some people in the hotel joined in congratulating me in a picture for me to keep as a memento. It was time for the bus to be driven away, so Mr Mowatt drove it forward and away to its parking place for the night. This must be almost the smallest bus depot in the Kingdom!

Mr Mowatt was a motor engineer and was in great demand for repair jobs among visiting motorists and he did not seem to be in the least surprised when he returned to find a young couple waiting with me for his return. They needed an inner tube for one of the car tyres. Our bus driver cum mechanic cum postman (for he was certainly that too) suggested that they might like to accompany us on a tour of Dunnet Head to see the Queen Mother's castle – and then he would see what he could do about helping them.

They seemed relieved at the thought of the help with the repair and quickly agreed that they would enjoy seeing the Castle of Mey, so the four of us settled in his car as we drove off to the west into the sunset.

It was not very far, a few miles – actually the castle is in the same parish as John O'Groats – and soon we were approaching a long avenue of trees that led to the gates, an avenue that seemed straight for nearly a mile.

Our best view was from the south, so we drove near a low wall where we could see the peat stack, which was used to keep the fires burning brightly through the winter. Mr Mowatt had a friend who was a gardener at the Castle and he told us about the green daffodils that grow in the garden in the spring and of the thousands of primroses which grow in the grasssy ditches almost down to the sea. A sight to see! We caught a glimpse of the fruit garden at the west side of the castle – although it was behind a high wall. The wall was an important factor in giving shelter to the trees by keeping out the high winds which blow in from the Arctic.

Cherry and plum blossom in spring would be a marvellous sight in the early sunshine with the blue of the sea and sky beyond them. No doubt there were apples, pears and other fruit besides and Mr Mowatt told us of the hot houses where luscious grapes hung in season. He called the Castle of Mey Barrogill, which has been the name for centuries, and after a while we found ourselves speaking of Barrogill Castle too. The old name lingers on even though it has Royal tenants.

The castle is dark grey and has many turrets – I counted 10 of them. Part of it has only two floors but the centre rises to four floors while the square turreted tower has five windows, one above the other, so this part would be five floors high. Inside, I was told of the steep narrow stairs up the little turrets.

'Those windows facing the garden are the library, and the windows on the first floor would be the big drawing room!'

'There's a view up there that must be well worth seeing!' I said. It would be a wonderful view of the Orkney Islands and Stroma to the north with Dunnet Head over to the west.

We were told of walls which were nine feet thick, and we ourselves could see the platforms and towers, battlements and turrets which make up this wonderful old castle. The winds were quiet as we left the Castle of Mey and the sun was dipping into the sea. It looked a little bit lonely.

I had had my wish – to see the Queen Mother's home, and now we were on our way back to John O'Groats, but before we arrived Mr Mowatt pointed out the Kirk of old Canisbay – the church with the tiny organ and little gallery where the Queen Mother goes to worship. There is no steeple just a square tower to the east, and it is surrounded by a thick stone wall. As we returned we could see the light of Dunnet Head Lighthouse sweeping round first over the mainland and then over the sea – and later, another lighthouse over to the east which I was told was Duncansby Head where the cliffs rise up sheer out of the sea and there are needle-like rocks standing away from them – the Stacks of Duncansby. I had thoroughly enjoyed the tour of the castle and the special places of interest nearby and now it was necessary for Mr Mowatt to go in search of a new tyre for our car-less friends. We made two journeys without success and on the third attempt, a new tyre was collected much to the satisfaction of the people with us.

I think Mr Mowatt was also making enquiries about accommodation for me at the same time, but he could not have been lucky, as I was still with him after our friends had gone. The new tyre had been fixed by the wayside and they left us looking decidedly more cheerful than when we met an hour before.

The lady of the party had been sitting next to me at the back of the car, while the gentlemen were busy on the repair job, and to pass the time away, she asked me about myself and my bus ride. I showed her some newspaper cuttings and when the men had finished the job and their car was about to leave she asked me if I would let her husband see the cuttings too.

'Of course, you're welcome,' I said and passed them round.

'Housewife goes to John O'Groats . . . ' her husband read the cuttings out loud much to the amusement of Mr Mowatt.

They pretended to congratulate me . . . not on the bus trip but on being a housewife to get into the papers!

It was on this cheery note that we said goodbye and saw them off on the rest of their holiday tour.

'You can come back with me,' suggested Mr Mowatt, 'we've plenty of room,' I thanked him for his kindness and he drove home. Out to 'Broo' which is named because it stands on the brow of the hill out on a sandy strip running along the shore. It must have been a tiny hill because to me the landscape looked flat as a pancake or a desert plain.

It was getting late when we reached the Mowatt home but the sunset lingered on. He drove the car round to a garage at the back of the house and I followed him past a long stack of peat which was as tall as my 5ft 4in. Cutting the peats from the peat bog had been his holiday job he told me. We went down a path made of slabs of slatey stone and into the warmth of the house. A giant white geranium stood inside the little square hall, and I noticed a telephone in the corner.

A door led off to the left into a large living room where his father was sitting and there were visitors who rose to go after greeting Mr Mowatt. He introduced me to the company and they left.

I stood back a little, while his father looked puzzled. No doubt he wondered who I was and how I came to be there . . . away up in John O'Groats . . . without an escort or companion, and without a car.

'It's Mrs Leather, Father!' said Mr William Mowatt. 'It's Mrs Leather, she's coom by bus' . . . and when his Father made no comment, he repeated, 'It's alreet Father, she's a *hooswife* . . . she'll wash t'dishes.'

All was well.

His father rose with a smile, and shook hands. 'Make yersel a cup o'tay. Make yersel at home!' was what he said.

Chapter 9

The dialect in John O'Groats was unlike any other that I had heard in Scotland and I noticed that although Mr William Mowatt spoke to me in English, he talked quite differently to his father. It was like a foreign language.

I am from a family who have their roots in East Anglia (Norwich) and my father has blue eyes and his hair – before it went grey – was fair. My father might have been sitting in that chair by the peat fire, Mr Daniel Mowatt looked so much like him. His build and everything about him made him look like *my* father.

Who knows? We probably both stem from the Vikings of Norway who came over centuries ago and set up homes on the pleasant shores of Scotland – I've heard about them.

Anyway I got along famously with them and soon felt at home.

We talked and Mr Mowatt – the driver – checked the bus tickets and made out a fares list as follows:

Whitton to Hounslow	4d
Hounslow to Slough	1s 2d
Slough to Maidenhead	1s 2½d
Maidenhead to Reading	1s 8d
Reading to Oxford	3s 10d
Oxford to Stratford	4s 9d
Stratford to Birmingham	2s 6d
Birmingham to Derby	3s 10d
Derby to Buxton	4s 6d
Buxton to Manchester	3s 2d
Manchester to Preston	3s 6d
Preston to Lancaster	1s 9d
Lancaster to Bowness	2s 11d
Bowness to Windermere	3d
Windermere to Ambleside	6d
Ambleside to Keswick	1s 10d
Keswick to Carlisle	3s 5d
Carlisle to Glasgow	10s 9d
Glasgow to Stirling	2s 2d
Stirling to Inverness	16s 9d
Inverness to Invergordon	3s 5d
Invergordon to Helmsdale	6s 9d
Helmsdale to Wick	4s 9d
Wick to John O'Groats	2s 0d
Unattributable ticket	8d
	£4 5s 9½d

He read out the 32 signatures on the schedule and was interested in the places I had passed through, asking several questions about the route.

We looked at the map together and he told me that I would enjoy going across Scotland another way – for my return journey – particularly if I could get across from Inverness to Fort William via the Caledonian Canal and the Great Glen. He told me that I should be able to get through to Glasgow from Fort William without any trouble and suggested that I enquire at MacBrayne's office in Inverness.

We sat around the peat fire and talked, but not for very long. There was a meal to get, and the kitchen to clear.

This was a bachelor establishment with books, newspapers and a wireless in the corner. The room was full of clocks – there was a tall grandfather clock standing by one wall, two on a cabinet, another on the mantlepiece, and another one on the window sill. I think Daniel Mowatt made a hobby of repairing clocks.

I went into the kitchen to help with the supper. It looked out on to a walled-in yard and there was an enormous boiler standing on one side. I gathered that this was used for water storage, but I am not sure.

There was a pail full of eggs under some shelves and another full of fish. There were crocks, and pots and pans of all description around, and they did not look as if they lacked very much.

The peat fire gave out a lovely warmth and heated the water. There was electric light and, as I have already mentioned, there was a telephone.

We had supper together and I was shown to my room after a little while. It was on the ground floor and looked out to the lighthouse on the east coast. There were plenty of blankets with which I made my bed.

The room was full of books and for a moment I was tempted to find one to read, but instead I asked William Mowatt if I might go outside for a moment to see the lights from the lighthouse. There was utter silence as I stood out of doors watching the tiny lights to the northeast. It swung out and round, giving a sweep of light at regular intervals, shining for a brief second in my direction, and then it was gone.

I looked to the south, over what would be a windswept plain, but could see nothing, nor could I hear a sound. There was no wind tonight, nor were there any trees to give a murmer of a breeze.

I spent a few moments in silent contemplation and turned to watch the light again for a few minutes before going back inside. I returned to the cosy atmosphere of the room and said goodnight to my hosts and then went to my room.

The cool air and sweet sunshine and the joy of the day left me feeling pleasantly tired, and I think I was soon asleep. My last impression was of the tiny light from the lighthouse passing across the window panes in the darkness. This was the turning point of my journey. Tomorrow, I would be starting back. I would leave when the bus went and as the driver was under the same roof, I should have to leave with him.

A 'note' for my schedule: remember to pick up the heather if Inspector Grant had been able to get me any. I had, therefore, to look in at Dingwall bus station beside the railway.

There was plenty of time in the morning for a leisurely look round, as the bus did not leave until 10 o'clock so I wandered round the house looking for a 'souvenir'. I found it in the form of a tiny bit of peat – surely as real a bit of Scotland as the heather. It is dark brown like wood and yet it is chunky like coal, and I had seen for myself what a lovely fire it makes. It burns with a hot glow and Mr Mowatt told me that the fire is kept in for weeks at a time. It is cut from the peat bog – like turf – and is left in the open to dry and harden.

'Take this for a souvenir!' suggested Mr William Mowatt, giving me a whisky bottle with the registered trade mark 'John O'Groats' on the label. I thanked him for it and turned it over in my hand to read the yellow label on the other side:

John O'Groats
In the year 1495 John de Groat, and his two brothers, natives of Holland, landed in Caithness bearing letters of recommendation from James IV King of Scots. Having obtained lands, by Royal Charter, in the parish of Canisbay, they prospered and were held in esteem by the people of Caithness.

In course of time, by the increases of their families, there came to be eight different landowners of the name of Groat. To celebrate the anniversary of the arrival of the family in Scotland, and annual festive gathering was established, and on one of these occasions a dispute arose as to who should take the door and sit at the head of the table.

In the interest of peace, John de Groat had to solve this question of precedency at their next annual meeting. To this end he built a house with eight doors and windows, in which was placed an octagonal table. By this means each man entered at his own door and sat at the head of the table, thereby complete harmony was restored.

This historic house has given the name to the district on the mainland of Scotland, which is far famed as the most northerly place on the mainland of Scotland, and the ultimate destination of motorists and tourists. The phrase 'from Lands End to John O'Groats' denotes a journey from one end of Great Britain to the other.

'And the flagstaff up by the hotel is the original site of the eight-sided house!' said Mr Mowatt.

I thanked him for my souvenirs and asked him if there was anything that I could send him from London to thank him for his kindness and hospitality. He thought he would like to have some of my photographs, so we added to them by taking some more pictures of him and his father at home for me to send to him.

The stack of peat fascinated me, so he took a picture of me beside the peat to show my family and friends. This is a real Highland touch . . . as genuine a one as you could find.

By now it was time to leave, so I collected my knapsack and said farewell to Daniel Mowatt, thanking him for his kindness in making me feel so much at home with them.

I left the quiet beauty of John O'Groats reluctantly, and walked with William Mowatt through the empty road to where the bus was parked. While he was getting it out, I went into the gift shop to buy a present for my daughter. The shop had a clean newness about it as though it had only recently been opened. I counted three houses around in this unique village – there would be space for a thousand more!

The bus appeared and I got in, taking a farewell look at the whitewashed walls of the 'Last house in Scotland' as it moved away.

In a distant field I could see someone rolling up a tent. The wide sandy road stretched now to the south . . . and although it was 600 miles away, I was on the way home.

I was sitting on top of the world. William Mowatt signed my schedule with date and the words. 'Bus departed John O'Groats 10am. And the best of luck.'

Above:
Large numbers of Alexander's famous Bluebird Coronation coaches of 1937 were still giving front line service in the mid-1950s. Seen here is WG 5487 (P351) with its Alexander body embellished with twin horns and flags on the radiator. *Robert Grieves Collection*

Below:
Mrs Leather made her journey from Glasgow to Inverness with a break at Stirling overnight but was in any case eschewing coach services. Of interest nonetheless is this view of a W & G operated on a Glasgow-Perth-Inverness service by Highland Motorways, a Glasgow-based firm, in 1928 shortly before the Alexander service was begun. *Robert Grieves Collection*

Above left:
An Alexander Bristol LS in Tay Street, Perth, in 1955 – the year it entered service and six years before it passed to Alexander (Fife). *Edward Shirras*

Above:
Standing at Perth station is the first of the Burlingham-bodied AEC Regal 1s delivered in 1946. *Edward Shirras*

Below left:
Perth local service buses wore a red livery as does this ex-London Transport Guy Arab which is actually seen in Dundee waiting to leave for its home base. Behind it is one of the PA class Leyland Tiger PS1s. *Edward Shirras*

Below:
Beside the River Tay in Tay Street, Perth, is Alexander P838, one of the Leyland Tiger TS7s dating from 1937 which were transferred from the Dundee area of Scottish Motor Traction in December 1949. *Edward Shirras*

Left:
Another vehicle on the stand in Tay Street is G99, one of the Guy-bodied Guy Arab IIIs. It passed in due course to Alexander (Fife). *Edward Shirras*

Below left:
Seen here in Pitlochry is P567, a Leyland Tiger TS8 new in April 1939. It remained in service for transfer to Alexander (Midland) in 1961 but was in fact withdrawn from service that year. *Edward Shirras*

Above right:
Operating on the summer service from Pitlochry to Ballater, an Alexander Bedford has a comfort stop in Braemar. *Edward Shirras*

Right:
Early in 1955 Highland Omnibuses obtained four Leyland Tiger TS7 buses formerly operated by Central SMT. The Leyland bodies had been rebuilt by Eastern Coach Works in 1951 but still showed the cutaway rear door fashionable when they were delivered in 1937. VD 7371, seen in Farraline Park bus station, Inverness was Highland H6. *Ian Maclean*

Below:
With a considerable expansion of workers' services in its area and more particularly in Caithness, from 1954 onwards Highland added to the double-deckers in its fleet. Among them was Park Royal-bodied Guy Arab II E87 which had been London Transport G116. After some 18 months the bus was withdrawn in 1954 when its chassis was, together with those of 17 other ex-LT vehicles, modified by Scottish Omnibuses and given a 30ft body. *Edward Shirras*

Above:
One of the revamped Guy Arabs was Highland K87 (KSC 919) seen here in the garage in Inverness. *Edward Shirras*

Right:
Inverness – a modern scene. *Scottish Tourist Board*

Below:
The Scottish Region branch to Dornoch from The Mound lingered on until 1960 but was not observed by Mrs Leather. The 10.25am from Dornoch is seen between Cambusavie Platform and The Mound. The 0-4-4T engine was in 1955 one of the two remaining Highland Railway steam locomotives which were retained to meet the weight restrictions on the branch. *C. E. Smith*

Above:
The 10.40am from Inverness to Wick and Thurso leaves The Mound hauled by Stanier Black 5 No 45138.
Ian Allan Collection

Below:
The signpost at Helmsdale showing also part of the back of

the 1943 Bedford OWB which had been rebuilt and reseated.
G. R. Leather

Below:
The bus from Invergordon to Helmsdale was A73, an Albion PW141 with a Cowieson body which had been rebuilt by Highland Transport. It was withdrawn in 1957.
G. R. Leather

Left:
The view ahead on the road from Wick to John O'Groats photographed on a later visit by Mrs Leather when William Mowatt was driving C17, one of the Bedford OWBs which Highland had converted to forward control and rebodied by Duple. *G. R. Leather*

Below left:
An out-of-period view, this picture nonetheless shows CD13, a Bedford VAM mailbus of Highland with Alexander bodywork negotiating a difficult corner at Latheronwheel on its way from Helmsdale to Wick.

Right:
After arrival at John O'Groats Highland driver William Mowatt and Mrs Leather pose in front of Bedford OWB C24 which entered the Highland fleet in September 1952 when the business of W. J. Mowatt Brothers was taken over. The bus had entered service with R. S. Waters of Wick in 1944.
G. R. Leather

Below:
Alexanders was a pioneer of extended touring in Scotland and this scene shows Walter Alexander Senior at the wheel of a solid-tyred Leyland charabanc at John O'Groats in 1920. This was a marathon venture for that period and a contemporary newspaper report of the journey described country folk along the route 'hiding in fear' as the vehicle **passed**! *Robert Grieves Collection*

Left:
John O'Groats. *Scottish Tourist Board*

Below left:
Helmsdale. *Scottish Tourist Board*

Below:
Furthest north of the Highland Omnibus garages was Thurso to which was attached in the mid-1950s a Duple-bodied Bedford OWB which had been taken over in October 1946 from Wilson (Royal Hotel), Thurso. Behind C8 (SK 2862) is a Guy Arab II with Northern Counties lowbridge body (E20: AST 958). *Ian Maclean*

Bottom:
New to Plymouth Corporation in January 1936 and bought by Alexander in November 1945 this Leyland Titan TD4 was rebodied by Alexander three months later – it had been re-engined before entering Alexander service. R555 which is seen about to leave Elgin for Inverness survived to pass to Alexander (Northern) in 1961 but was withdrawn soon afterwards. *Edward Shirras*

Above:
Another view of Highland E20, one of the first two double-deckers to operate in Caithness where it appeared in 1946. *J. Campbell Collection*

Above:
In Farraline Park bus station about to leave Inverness for Macduff is Alexander K66, one of 85 Leyland Cheetahs delivered in 1938. It was given an oil engine in January 1946. When the division of the fleet came in 1961 only 11 remained for transfer of which eight went to Fife and three to Midland. *Edward Shirras*

Left:
A later bus on the Wick-John O'Groats service which is seen standing beside the Highland Wick garage was this Bedford VAS1 with Duple Midland body. CD2 was delivered in 1964.

Below:
Alexander Leyland Lion LT5B P167 was one of a batch of 30 delivered in 1934 which had six-cylinder Leyland 8.6litre oil engines from the outset but unlike many of the batch it did not receive a new body. It is seen at Elgin with Inverness on the blind. *Edward Shirras*

Part 2

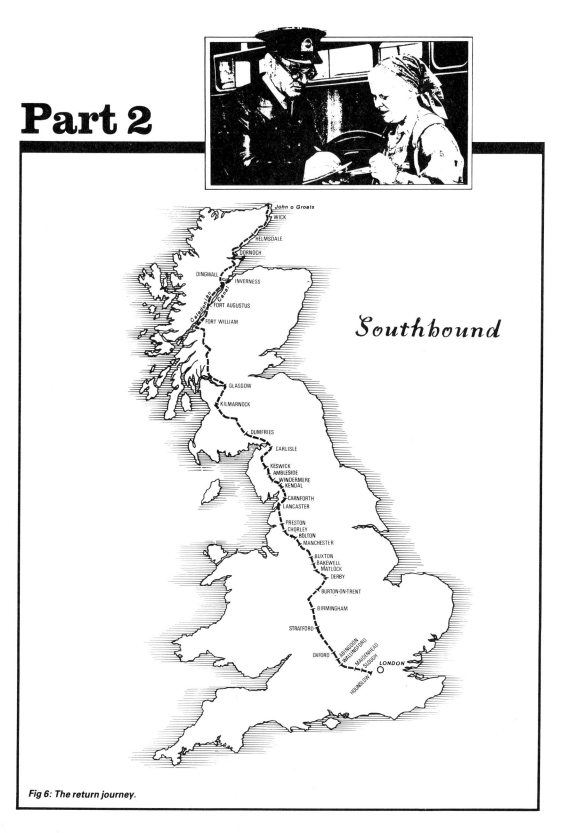

Fig 6: *The return journey.*

Chapter 10

In many ways I thought the journey along the east coast, at least as far as Dornoch, would be a repetition of what I had already seen. There would be a series of tiny villages lying like a string of pearls beside the sea. But the aspect, coming south, looked considerably less forbidding, much less austere in the clear morning light. The sun shone on vegetation crushed and beaten by the storms over the coast and there was a quiet beauty about it which I could appreciate. I hated to leave this wide sweep of country with its air of extreme solitude to return to the bustle of the towns. The distance from John O'Groats to Wick – 22 miles – took just over an hour, and the bus pulled up near the Highland Omnibus office at 11.15am. I took leave of William Mowatt thanking him for his kindness and hospitality and found a little place near the Post Office where I could get a cup of coffee, leaving my belongings in the cafe for a while as there was time for a look round before the next bus.

Wick is essentially a fishing harbour and the shops looked bright and busy. Before leaving I went back to the cafe to pick up my things and bought some sandwiches and chocolate for the journey, and wrote a few postcards to let the family know I was on the way home. Wick seemed very self-contained as though it was quite capable of taking care of itself.

The bus for Helmsdale appeared on the bridge at Wick about one o'clock – a small Highland Omnibus and I took my seat among the shoppers. I wondered what my neighbour would have said had I told her that I was on my way to London by bus! I had a return ticket for this part of the journey and Miss Jean Dunnett – the lady conductor – was kind enough to sign my schedule for me and told me that the distance to Helmsdale was about 40 miles . . . with the sea for company the whole way. The sun sparkled on the waves near the shore and away in the distance there was a slight haze over the sea. It was a beautiful sight from the windows of the bus. Floating near the shore I could occasionally see a small boat tied to a post.

Looking in the other direction I could see small homes and a few sheep grazing over the rough grass. Near to the road were patches of peat bog and tufts of tiny windblown flowers, pale yellow and white. The bus stopped to take parcels and to deliver letters here and there along the Highland road at little cottage gates.

At one place a horse was tethered behind the wall, and he peered at the bus as though with some surprise and then wandered off.

I found a friend in a woman in a brown coat with a big shopping basket who was sitting behind me. She told me she had come north from Aberdeen with her husband and was just getting used to new lands and new folk. This strange point of view took me by surprise for surely it was all Scotland but she impressed on me that at first she had been as lonely as an exile.

The chimney pots of Helmsdale came into view and the bus pulled up on the bridge. My companion got up and bade me a pleasant journey, and left the bus.

The town of Helmsdale with which I was getting familiar – as this was where I had my longest wait on my way up – lies on a hillside above the harbour, and looks to the south over the North Sea. Just a handful of houses and shops, then over a stone bridge and you are in the open country again. Round the horns of land which enclose the harbour, the coast shows on either side a battlement of cliffs through which a burn or two makes its way through to the sea.

Then on to Dornoch, a distance of another 28 miles. My schedule was signed by Miss Jenny Cumming and we reached the lovely old town just before six o'clock. The bus stopped in a wide open space in front of a building that was imposing enough to have been a castle, but I was told that it was used as a barracks.

There was time to get out of the bus and look around, and again I was attracted to lovely bushes of scented honeysuckle in nearby gardens. The wide forecourt in front of the grey stone walls looked just the place for a gathering of Highlanders, and one to which the sound of pipes must have been very familiar.

Before reaching Dornoch we had passed through the Duke of Sutherland's estates, and there I had seen a delightful handicraft shop full of tartan shawls and Scottish souvenirs and gifts. The shop itself was intriguing too, built of tall fir trees roughly hewn and sawn to size. The wooden porch was hung with Border tweeds and tartan scarves and was a bright spot in the heart of the otherwise sombre fir tree countryside.

I was reminded of it by a lady on the bus who showed me a piece of Celtic jewelry – a grouse claw made into a brooch which she wore to pin down her Shetland scarf. I wished that I could have bought souvenirs of my visit like these but I had to be content with seeing them in their native surroundings. I was satisfied that I was seeing a place where nature was at its loveliest, and the people at their friendliest. Never did I lack someone to talk to, if I felt so inclined, and I met with courtesy and pleasantness everywhere.

From Dornoch I had to go on to Inverness where I planned to spend the night. This was a distance of another 75 miles but first I had to make sure of calling at Dingwall.

This was no time to doze. Still on the coast road with the sea all the way, we travelled on, through Tain and Invergordon and pulled up near the railway station at Dingwall; and although I did not see Inspector Grant again, he had left a pail full of beautiful heather just inside the doorway. I thanked the people on duty and gathered it up into my arms, and left a message to be passed on to the thoughtful inspector who had remembered, and returned to the bus ahead of the conductor.

It sounds a very long way but at no time did I find the journey boring as there was so much to see. The grandeur of the hills and the beauty of sylvan glens followed by stretches of forest where you had to look straight up to see the sky, was surely enough to keep anybody awake and it was only after hours and hours of seeing so much natural beauty that my mind could not absorb any more, and I would relax and doze, confident that the same beautiful scenery would be there when I woke.

And so the day went by and it was about four hours after Dornoch that I reached Inverness. It was too dark to see more than the outline of the famous old castle when I arrived, and I was fortunate to find a room immediately beneath the walls of the castle, at Bain's Hotel in Castle Street. Here I had supper, bed and breakfast. The hotel was run by Mr Alex Munro, the accommodation was very comfortable and the bill a modest one.

There was no time for dawdling in the morning but I did have a few moments in which to see the Stone of the Tubs. It is to one side of the Town Hall, and is famous for its connection with history, so I was told by a policeman who was nearby. My own interest lay in the fact that its name came from a more practical use! The womenfolk rested their tubs on it as they carried their weekly wash back and forth from the river. They must have been grateful for a little rest by the wayside.

The High Street is wide and the shops were getting busy for the day when I made my way to MacBraynes's office for the next bus. The bus depot

was crowded, so I took my place in the queue along with holidaymakers, and soon our bus was pretty nearly packed with people and luggage. However we sorted ourselves out and as we sat down to make ourselves comfortable, I was surprised to find that there were even a few seats to spare. Most of the people I thought were in our queue had been waiting for other buses.

The bus was too sumptuous for my liking – I prefer air and space to heavy upholstery, but this was the only type used for the long journey across the Highlands and soon I was very appreciative of the comfortable seats. The castle at Inverness stands on a hill and can be seen for miles. Below is the River Ness, with hills rising up to Tomnahurich on the Caledonian Canal. I caught a glimpse of the cathedral and an attractive park as we wended our way through the town, and out on to the flat road which runs alongside Loch Ness.

It had been a very dry summer and in many places where there should have been water, it was just a flat expanse of drying mud. The Caledonian Canal had in some places dried up completely, at least that is how it looked from the bus, just a wide waste of land with trickles of water running in the shallow bed.

But nothing could take away the aspect of beauty from the road to the Great Glen – surely the most charming of all roads in the north.

I asked the conductor to sign my schedule when I paid for my ticket. The fare was £1 0s 6d which I think probably constitutes a record as being the highest price I have paid for a bus ticket. It was an 11s ticket over-printed with the words nine-six, and I noted the number with interest – Aa 6983. This would take me through from Inverness to Glasgow, via the Great Glen and Fort William, and I was told that I should have to change buses at a place called Kinlochleven.

The mere fact of getting such an expensive ticket and asking for his signature was enough to set my charming conductor talking. He smiled and said something to me in Gaelic – which of course I did not understand.

'You'll have to write it down!' I said, handing him a pencil and the back of an envelope. 'I'll never remember all that – and what is more I should like to!'

And this is what he wrote for me – 'Ceud Mille Falch' – Gaelic for a Hundred Thousand Welcomes.

Then in English he added, 'I trust you are having an enjoyable journey!' I thanked him for his interest and told him that I had really been having a wonderful time and that I just could not take in so much lovely scenery all the time, there was so much of it to see.

He told me that he sung at the Gaelic Festival which is known as the 'Lochaber Provincial Mod.' It is held every year at Fort William and competitors come from all over the Highlands.

I asked him what he sang, and he told me that the name of the song that he sang this year was 'Mo Chruinneag Ileach' which translated means 'My Islay Maiden'. He told me that he was very interested in music, that his name was William F. Grigor and that he lived in Glenurquhart which is in Inverness-shire.

The whole morning was taken up by the journey from Inverness to Fort William and I do not think I have ever seen more beautiful scenery than through the heather clad mountains of the Great Glen.

The conductor passed round little booklets which helped us to know the places we were passing through, so from it I can mention a few of them. Loch End, Loch Ness, Drumnadrochit, and into the shelter of the hills of Invermoriston took us along the road above the Caledonian Canal to Fort Augustus. The bus made several stops along the way to pick up passengers but in all those miles there was only a handful of people.

We passed a few forestry cottages and in some places tree felling was in progress. The trees towered up into the sky and had grown so closely together that peering into them was like looking into a dark cathedral.

Occasionally we would pass what looked like a small petrified forest. Here the trees had been cut down and carried away and the stumps had weathered to a greyish white and lay about forlorn and dejected.

On the far side of the water, the hilly ranges extended the whole way through the Glen in all shades of greys and purple browns, lime green and lovely blues. A wonderful sight full of beauty and interest.

In front of me, for some time, sat an elderly gentleman and a young boy. The man included me and my seat companion when he talked to the boy, telling him the points of interest along the way.

He told us that the road had been built so that a whole army of troops could march along them and they provided the first good roads in the Highlands. Previously deer tracks and stony mountain paths were used for exploring the byways through the hills and they must have been lonely indeed. Among the places he pointed out to us on the route included the boathouse used by John Cobb and the measured mile marked by white posts at Loch Ness. This was where John Cobb lost his life during his attempt on the world water speed record in September 1952. It was a beautiful stretch of water to have such a sad association.

The old bridge and falls of Invermoriston and nearby the watching house, where fishermen can watch salmon going up the falls were all pointed out to me – as were Orch Bridge and the power house for the hydro-electric scheme at Invergarry where the rushing water is put to practical use. Behind us lay Fort Augustus on the edge, so to speak, of Loch Ness and beside ran the Caledonian Canal. As we were in the middle of a very dry summer, the water was very shallow and we could see the pebble and rock bed of the canal in many places as we went along. It looked pink and grey in the sunlight.

The gentleman told me that during the 19th century the three Lochs – Loch Ness, Loch Oich and Loch Lochy – were joined together with an artificial cutting to make the Caledonian Canal.

I summoned up enough courage to tell him that I did not understand the meaning of the word 'Loch' and he charmingly explained that it was quite simple. Loch was the Scottish word for lake, and Scotland was the land O'Lakes or Land O'Lochs. I told him that the title was pretty, and he smiled.

'Woman!' he said, 'it's more than that it's *beautiful!*'

The more I saw of Scotland the more I agreed with him. We looked at the trees silhouetted against the heather-coloured hills, and the rocks mirrored in the water, and it looked calm and peaceful – as still and lovely as a painting. I told him of my travels by buses, and how much I had seen.

He expressed keen interest and agreed with me that you could see more, much more, from a bus than from the finest car on the road.

'Your idea is grand' he said. 'It's simple – it's so simple as to be almost idiotic. I like it! Why we could all be travellers like that.'

We talked for a while, and then he went back to his role of guide and pointed out to us the Commando Memorial which was unveiled by the Queen in 1954. This was the Commando War Memorial at Spean Bridge, Inverness-shire to the men who fought to preserve our freedom. Below, ran the River Spean and the road made a sharp bend as we approached the bridge.

The hills had given place to a wide expanse of rough grass, and we saw a number of shaggy Highland cattle roaming near the road.

'This would be the beginning of the Great Glen Cattle Ranch – Fine Scotch Beef!'

We all looked at the big Highland cattle with their great horns and the cattle stared back at us, as if the bus was the most interesting thing they had seen.

'Used to be sheep here, but sheep are no good for the land. Now the grass is greener and in better condition, and the stock has been increased in these last 10 years,' said our informant.

The sun was shining over the yellow cattle station and the low hills, and not unnaturally I thought of roast beef and Yorkshire pudding, for it was getting close to lunchtime. I wondered when the opportunity would come for the next meal.

But all thoughts of food vanished in the next few minutes when through the open window of the bus came the lovely smell of wood smoke. A curling wisp of blue smoke drifted up the glen from somewhere among the pines and was caught in the funnel of air beside the bus. We all sniffed hard.

If the moorland scents were delicious, the breath of forest smoke was quite ravishing. Smells mean a lot to us, though our tastes may differ.

'I love the smell of bacon and eggs,' said the boy.

'Umm – I prefer the smell of new bread!' said the elderly gentleman. New books, leather harness, apples in store and the scent of ferns in the sun, or hoar frost on the hills – between us, we loved them all.

Over all this lovely road through the Highlands, there had been the smell of heather in the sun, and the scent of the pine and fir trees. Up over the heights too, the air had a delightful clean tang about it as it came to us through the windows of the bus. Away ahead, the road shone in the morning light, and rocks of every hue – from palest pink to grey and mauve and mossy green stood up along the edges of the road and seemed to point the way.

I spoke of the rocks to my seat companion and she said that they had a practical value too. They helped to mark the road during the winter when the snows came and the road would be in danger of being obliterated.

'The snow drifts can be very dangerous, and the rocks are a permanent guide,' she pointed out.

On our right we were still travelling past the open range where the cattle wandered, and soon we saw the big name sign of the Great Glen Cattle Ranch. We might have been in the cattle country of America, it seemed so remote to me and so unlike what I might have expected to see from a bus! However, I had seen so much, that I was no longer surprised at the wonder of my journey, and just looked and looked, taking in every detail that I could. I was exploring the lonely, almost uninhabited part of the Highlands, and the peace and quiet of it all was very satisfying. We were by now about 60 miles from our starting point at Inverness and judging by our little map of the route which our conductor had given us, we were nearing Ben Nevis – the highest mountain in the Highlands, and incidently, running downhill into Fort William.

There were so many peaks along the range of hills that although I looked hard, I could not be sure which one was Ben Nevis. However the bus conductor made sure that we all saw the big mountain, and the bus too, helped by travelling slowly as it crept downward to the town, and eventually I felt that I had my eyes in the right direction and could see the rounded shoulders of Ben Nevis standing out above those of the peaks surrounding it.

I was told that on a clear day it is possible to see the northern tip of Ireland from the heights of Ben Nevis and that climbers take up a map with them in order to identify the distant mountain peaks and the lochs and waterfalls that nestle between the hills.

For myself I had to be satisfied with seeing all the varied colours of the hilly range – the greys and mauves and green – and with wondering whether the white patches which I could see near the top might be drifts of ice and snow. The conductor suggested the idea to us, but no-one could be sure.

The bus continued the journey downhill in the broiling sun, with the road twisting and turning, and suddenly we were pulling up in Fort William outside the bus office near the ferry.

It had been a wonderful morning with all the places of the Highlands in every minute. But now the quiet scene had changed, as if some hand had waved a magic wand.

There were people everywhere, a crowd of holiday makers and a queue of cars slowly coming down the winding hill on one side and making their way up the other.

With the rest of the passengers, I got down from the bus with my heather and luggage, and walked up the busy street in search of lunch. We stopped to thank the conductor for his kind assistance and said goodbye to each other.

I took a quick look at the ferry boat which was waiting for passengers who would be going to Camusnagaul and then turned towards the town.

Chapter 11

Now I was in the Scotland of the visitors, a place with a warm heart and a welcome for the tourist. The shops were full of tartans and hand woven tweeds, bright socks and scarves, beautiful leather goods and delightful jewellery. I wanted to shop and look at everything, but first I had to make sure of some lunch.

There were so many cafes and restaurants to choose from all with lovely Scottish names – Fraser's, Cameron's, the Clansman – that I would have liked to have sampled them all, but as you may guess, I walked into the nearest.

Fort William was unexpected after so many miles of mountain scenery. The contrast too, was refreshing, for here was the wealth of Scotland in a different form.

I had a light lunch and some delicious coffee, and then I hurried up the High Street to visit some of the shops. I really don't know how I resisted some of those fascinating treasures. I touched a whisper soft Shetland shawl to see the price tag and thought how lovely it would have been to take home. It was as airy as gossamer but beautifully warm to the touch – ties in clan tartans too were particularly attractive.

Then I saw a novelty that I had not the heart to pass by – delicious little handkerchiefs embroidered with the flowers of the Highland Clans . . . myrtle, thistle, rowanberries, and tiny flowers of the forest all worked in fine stitches each one a picture.

I bought what I could afford, and talked to the assistant, asking the price of tartan silk purses and belts which had also caught my eye. The shoulder brooches, dirks, tam-o-shanters, Balmoral and Glengarry caps, and other charming Scottish traditional things were displayed with tartan kilts and homespun tweeds and attracted me with their colour and good quality.

But time was short and soon I had to make my way back to the bus.

I stood again for a few moments looking at the ferry and gazed into the distance at the blue hills beyond. Then back to my bus which would take me on the long journey to Glasgow. I felt that I had made the most of my time at Fort William and enjoyed my interlude at this tourist centre among the lochs. I did not hear the sound of bagpipes – except in the back of my mind.

The High Street was warm in the noonday sun as I made my way to a little gathering of people by the buses. Here I saw Mr Grigor who told me that the same bus would be going on to a place called Kinlochleven, but that the crew changed here, and he would be going back to Inverness. By this method the bus drivers and conductors get back home instead of being carried further and further away.

I had my camera in my hand, as I had been taking pictures of the ferry and excursion boats, so I asked Mr Grigor if I could take a picture of him with the bus to add to my souvenirs. When my roll of film was used up, I said farewell to Fort William and to him and took my seat on the sunny side of the bus for another long journey. It was now one o'clock and taking it in easy stages I should be in Glasgow about six o'clock.

My former companions had gone, and I resorted to the map for information about the next part of the route to add to what I could see from the bus.

As we left Fort William we had a much better view of Ben Nevis, and the neighbouring mountains. Ben Nevis (their own Big Ben) is the highest mountain in the country, 4,406ft high, and the track climbers use is about two miles out of Fort William. Macbeth is reputed to have died in a castle whose ruins stand on an island in the hills of Glen Nevis.

The lower half is composed of red granite with grey volcanic rocks above, and then a smooth table of rock at the very top. At certain times of the year there is a race from the town of Fort William to the top of 'the Ben', as it is affectionately called, and the record time for the race, there and back, is under two hours. I could just imagine those climbers trying to find the short cuts instead of following the track!

My last look on Ben Nevis was seeing it framed by the trees as we neared the bridge at Coruanan. We were now on our way to the famous Glencoe Pass and the little villages as we passed on the way seemed to be hiding among the trees. They were so tiny compared to the rolling hills and mountains all around as to be almost invisible, except for their whitewashed walls. We could see the road winding for miles ahead, while near at hand beautiful birch trees with their silver-grey bark and graceful foliage rustling in the lightest of breezes made pictures for us that afternoon that I shall always remember.

The sun was now on my face, and just then there was no escaping it and I must have dozed off for I woke with the sudden stopping of the bus.

We were at Kinlochleven about 12 miles out of Fort William, and everyone was getting out! It seemed a nice place, so I collected my heather and my belongings and joined the throng outside the bus. There were shops and houses and several groups of people waiting. But there was nothing to worry about – we were merely changing buses.

In about 10 minutes we were settled on another bus moving slowly down the road out of Kinlochleven and shortly afterwards were travelling steadily along the road to Glencoe which, according to my little guide map, was built by German prisoners during World War 1.

The land slopes sharply from vast grey-green mountains into the little glen and I kept turning my head this way and that as fresh views came into sight – of barren peaks and rocky headlands that were like a picture postcard of a scene rather than the scene itself.

Great peaks with areas of flat grassland as valleys between, will have to become names but I wish I could show you that 'top of the world' spot as I saw it.

Another bus had stopped on the road ahead, and we pulled up behind it, but apart from the passengers, it was the loneliest place you could imagine. Here we were to have a few minutes respite – whether to cool off the engine after a long climb or purely for the passengers to view the scenery I do not know, but we all got out and stretched our legs and walked around over the short dry heather.

The conductor pointed out Buchaille Etive Mhor – a granite-like peak ahead – and Glen Etive below. He told me that this was a favourite spot for climbers, but what caught my eye was a sign pointing out 'Mountain Rescue Kit at Altnafeagh – 2 miles,' which seemed somewhat ominous.

I know very little about Scottish history but there were many around me who were anxious to explain the connections these beautiful places had with the past. I heard about the MacDonalds and the massacre of 1692. This was the Valley of the Shadow of Death. Perhaps this was the real reason for the lonely valley. To me it looked rather like a vast arena where a searchlight tattoo might be held – perhaps that is why I seemed to be listening for the distant sound of bagpipes from over the hills! The place seemed familiar to me as though I had seen it on a film with a great crowd of kilted Highlanders in some enthusiastic display. But the scene remained in my mind as a vast lonely place – quiet and peaceful.

Our handful of people were getting back on the bus, so I walked a few more steps away from them to pick a wee piece of heather that was growing beside a tiny trickle of a stream and for that reason was fresher looking than any other, then I too returned to the bus.

The ghosts of Glencoe moved out of the way to let the driver through the pass, and I noticed several people on the bus near me raise their chins and lift their eyes to the hills to see beyond the cloudless sky.

We had already passed the Three Sisters and gone through the Gorge before reaching Glencoe and if I remember rightly Rannoch Moor stretched away to the left of the bus. Several of the mountainous hills near here were over 3,000ft in height, and looked most impressive.

Some of these deeper, darker hills may have been 20-30 miles away but because of the light, which gives everything a particular brilliance, it looked as if you could easily walk to them. This must account for the fascination of the hills to climbers, the clearness making the effort look a good deal easier than it really is.

Sometimes the valleys between the hills lay in the shadow, but I could sometimes see wild flowers and dark tufty grasses growing, as though beside an invisible tumbling stream.

From my wonderful watchtower on the bus I could see the road disappearing ahead of us to the south with Loch Ba and Loch Tulla. Then came the glens with a road from Dalmally and Oban joining up with the one we were on at the Bridge of Orchy. Then down into Tyndrum and the junction with the main road from Oban. Here the bus pulled up for a while and there was time to get a quick cup of tea, which was very welcome. I met a young couple who told me that they had been spending their honeymoon fortnight at Oban visiting the isles of the sea. They were full of enthusiasm for all the places they had visited, and like me, had been blessed with the most glorious weather.

There was not time to tell them about my own journey, but they gasped with astonishment when I told them that I had brought a piece of peat with me from John O'Groats, and carried it all the way by bus. It was only a tiny piece, of course, but I showed it to them nevertheless as I felt it was a fitting souvenir to bring away from the peat bog country and they were most intrigued. I had to keep all my souvenirs small, as my big bouquet of heather from Sutherland was as much as I could manage.

After tea and cakes I rejoined the bus for the journey on to Crianlarich. Our driver and conductor had apparently also been away to have tea or light refreshment for they were a few minutes before making their appearance.

The road ran beside the waters of Fillon and Glen Falloch while in the distance we could see the peak of Ben Lui. There were small rivers and streams running towards us as the bus passed along the valley.

I was keenly aware of the beauty of the drive which I was enjoying immensely. In one place the bark of birch trees made a glittering splash of silver in the sunlight against Scots pine and Douglas fir trees with their contrasting rich green branches. In the foreground damp bracken near the water's edge looked like a carpet of golden brown. Over all this, an assortment of wild duck circled round before alighting on the water of the loch. What a delightful place for a picnic, I thought, as I noticed a parked car and a family of children in cotton frocks having tea near the water.

An elderly lady sitting in the back seat appeared to be enjoying herself 'just sitting' and watching the birds. The soil was rich, no doubt well watered with soft rain and soft sea mists on other days, but today was a day in a million with luminous sunshine, the very finest day of summer, and on my long slow tour from John O'Groats I seemed to be seeing every possible kind of scenery from the flat wide horizons of Caithness to the steep ridge provided by the mountains of the West. I had loved the strangeness of Caithness, the unusual character of this beautiful country and it was being emphasised more and more now that I was getting further away from it.

I fell to thinking of my journey towards John O'Groats and could not help wishing that I had stayed longer, and seen more of this remote part of the country while I was there. Well, it was no good wishing, for the bus was going south and I was really on my way home; I stopped looking back to enjoy instead the romantic hills and distant peaks of the present hour.

The sense of adventure returned as I realised that I had been travelling for seven days . . . and seven nights – for surely the spirit of adventure is with you even when you sleep, when you are enjoying a carefree holiday. Perhaps I was even now in the loveliest part of all Scotland. How difficult it is to say which place was the best – so much of it was too spectacular for the novice like me to describe.

All that I can say is, do not be deterred from a wonderful journey like this. Don't be put off. See this all for yourself one day – this rare beauty that is so difficult to describe.

I was lucky with the weather. I'll admit that we were having a long spell of glorious sunshine, and this had been the driest summer for many years, but even if I had encountered rain and mists and grey skies I think I should still have caught the spell of these magical highlands – the great heights and wild forests with bejewelled lakes adding to the mystery of the scene. Once seen, the beauty is never forgotten.

On to Ardlui, where the bus stopped at about half past three, and then to Tarbet, along the shores of lovely Loch Lomond for many, many miles. Another picturesque expanse of water and then we made for Inverberg. Within the shadow of whitewashed walls, cottagers were sitting out of the heat of the sun, and in the opposite direction reflected sunlight caught the edge of yet another loch, and made it sparkle like a necklace of diamonds.

It is somewhere near here that the hydro-electric scheme has changed the face of Scotland, with new buildings to house the generators, and new homes to house the workers, but as I did not see the place before the 'change' I was not very aware of the damage to the landscape.

I was becoming aware of the traffic on the road, now that we were getting nearer to Glasgow, and I reminded myself that it was 28 July and approaching the August Bank Holiday weekend. No doubt there would be thousands of cars on the road, but the procession lost itself in the distance – those going our way speeding past us and the traffic going in the opposite direction losing itself inconspicuously among the hills.

I was able to return to my reverie and in quiet reflection among the hills and valleys the bus and I (with a few other quietly contented people) settled back to enjoy the last hour of the run.

The little map I have tells me that we passed the Coat of Arms Gate, the entrance to Rhossdhu House – the home of Sir I. Colquhoun, Chief of the Clan, but I only remember seeing the Colquhoun Hotel, so probably my attention was diverted to something else when we passed the gate.

I did notice a number of charming spots in and around Loch Lomond, so I probably saw the largest island in the loch which is called Inchmurren, but as the guide map says there are 22 islands in the loch, it would not be possible for me to be sure. Many of the islands seemed to be inhabited with houses that must have had wonderful views and the people in them are very fortunate to live amid such romantic scenery.

In a few cases there were noble castles that seemed to be built in the middle of lochs where the occupants could survey miles of pleasant water, with great rocks and the shadow of the hills to keep them company. Everywhere the air was redolent with the fragrance of pine trees, and the colours changed to cinnamon with the turn of the road, always rich and varied and always beautiful.

My guide map tells me that we passed the Vale of Leven industrial estate at Bonhill and Dumbuck Hill, a few miles south as we drove out of Dunbartonshire into Lanarkshire. I must have been chatting with a neighbour because I do not remember them. Soon I began to realise we were leaving incredibly lovely mountain scenery and were driving into the outskirts of Glasgow. There seemed to be no more hills or valleys, but instead one looked out on four-storied houses, factories and offices.

The road widened considerably and we passed a large shipyard where the liners *Queen Mary* and *Queen Elizabeth* had been built and huge cranes towered into the sky. Somewhere near I heard the hooter of a factory, and we crossed and recrossed bridges over the River Clyde.

It was six o'clock, and I had arrived in Glasgow. I gathered up my bag and heather and left the bus.

Chapter 12

I quickly realised that I must make a rapid readjustment if I was to stay alive long enough to enjoy my evening in Glasgow. After the quiet and peace of the Highlands, and the protected seclusion of the bus, I was suddenly plunged into the noise and uproar of a great city at holiday time. I walked out of the bus depot, dodged out of the way of a tram, evaded several fast-moving cars and found a cafe where I could have a cup of tea, to take stock of my position.

One of the first things to be done was to let some people on the Scottish newspapers, who had been interested in my journey, know that I had arrived in Glasgow. Checking that I had all my bus tickets together, and my schedule handy, I decided to find the place I wanted by walking through the city. After so much sitting, I could do with a good stretch. Suiting the action to the word, I stretched muscles and limbs like a cat preparing to take a leap. Then I shouldered my few belongings, retied my bouquet of heather and strode out into the main road to ask my way. The evening was warm and there were bright lights all the way.

I need not have worried about taking in Glasgow. Glasgow took me by the hand and I loved it! The newspaper people were pleased that I had looked them up and I was introduced to some very charming folk and invited to have supper with them. Their gaiety was quite infectious and I was thrilled to meet them. A photographer took my picture before I left them, and I showed them my collection of bus tickets and signed schedule of the journey. They complimented me on my perseverance and progress and listened attentively to my chatter, and a Mr Garbett offered to take me out to Hillhead where they thought I could find accommodation for the night. This turned out to be in the neighbourhood of the River Kelvin.

'This is outside the jungle of Glasgow,' said Mr Garbett. 'I hope you like it here.' It was an attractive place, a small hotel run by a Mr Russell Moreland, quiet and peaceful. Miss Jean King signed my schedule. I was offered tea and scones on a tray in the dining room, and was joined by a hefty young gentleman in corduroy shorts and a thick plaid shirt.

He talked English with a foreign accent, and I learnt that he was a student of marine engineering. He was very polite and obviously too young to have been in the war. He talked freely about himself and his parents in Germany and said that he was 'very lucky to be accepted in Glashgo!' I smiled and thought he was too – but I did not say anything. 'It is a wonderful atmosphere for a young man – and so stimulating – arguments are carried to the bitter end!' he said. Finally we said goodnight and he carried my tray out with his to the kitchen. I found a newspaper to read what had been happening while I had been on a slow tour of the north. Most of the paper seemed to be devoted to football, and it seemed strange to think that the names I had heard so many times on the radio on Saturday afternoons were teams with their playing fields not many miles from where I sat. I don't think I ever thought that these places existed before this moment – Motherwell and Queen of the South, Celtic and Partick Thistle.

There being nothing else to read, I went up to my room. I lay awake until midnight thinking of my wonderful journey and of my spontaneous welcome in Glasgow. In the morning the sunshine woke me up – it was going to be another lovely day. I had a bath after early tea in bed. From then onwards, I proceeded to enjoy my few hours in Glasgow before getting a bus to take me through southern Scotland and down to Carlisle. It may have been a brief visit, but I managed to see quite a lot of the character of the city. Glasgow was surprisingly quiet because it was the Friday of the bank holiday weekend, and no doubt a lot of people were on holiday.

Everyone I met was friendly and had an air of confidence that I found exhilarating. Walking up this road and that, I walked around the immediate vicinity of Hillhead until I thought I had better get to the centre of the city, if I wanted to see some of the places of interest. I took a 4d tram ticket to the neighbourhood of George Square which appeared to be central for the main post office and the municipal buildings as well as for several of the large railway stations – which I noted but, of course, on my journey would not need.

In the centre of George Square, I saw the monument to Sir Walter Scott, a massive column that no-one could pass without stopping to look at, while on all sides of the square there were statues to great men of the past. The air was brilliantly clear as I walked towards the University, where the birds were chirping their delight in the blue skies and pleasant sunshine. There was not time for me to go far afield. Glasgow is a huge place, and a great centre of industry, as well as being a starting point for thousands of tourists who are able to travel around the north and into the Highlands. I had to be satisfied with what I could see in a short time. Lunched on eggs and chips at 1.30pm, and then on to the bus station in Waterloo Street for another journey. This was obviously a big bus depot with a large waiting hall for the growing queues. There were no seats, and I was one of many who waited a long time. I began to wish for a seat and something to read but I could not risk my place in the queue. Perhaps the next time I go there the omnibus people will have put a few seats around the walls so that, at least, mothers with fidgety children can sit awhile. A newspaper kiosk would have done a roaring trade that day. Eventually, a bus inspector called for the passengers waiting for the Carlisle bus, and I went downstairs to join the bus. The bus garage was under the waiting hall, and we were soon on our way out of Glasgow, going south. It was three o'clock when we left and I was glad to be sitting down. We drove through city streets and past four-storied tenement houses, then into the suburbs where the houses had gardens and looked cheerful and bright, and finally I lay back and closed my eyes. I was tired from walking round and round – and seeing so much. Everything had been so interesting, and the time had gone so quickly, that I was glad to be back on a comfy seat again and just let myself be driven along quietly.

The bus stopped and started several times; we went through Kilmarnock and near the Burns countryside of Ayr. I have to admit that I don't know much about Robert Burns except that he wrote lovely poetry that is difficult to read because it is written in the dialect. We passed through Cummock, and now I was seeing the Lowland country. After the Highlands and the very northern parts this section of Scotland was not so attractive to me. There were solid little towns and farms that suggested a lot of hard working people.

I had been sitting on my own, until two very jolly girls brought me into their conversation, and then we all talked together. They had been on a hiking and bus riding holiday and were now on their way home to Haltwhistle, near Hexham in Northumberland, south of the border between England and Scotland. Their names were Miss Eileen Little and Mrs Agnes Hamilton – they were full of fun and obviously had a wonderful time. I was travelling from one end of the bus route to the other, from Glasgow to Carlisle, but they left the bus at Dumfries to pick up another going towards Hexham. It was then seven o'clock.

Dumfries was full of holiday crowds, and the bus parked for some time near cafes and sweet shops, and I took the opportunity to dash off and get an ice cream. In the two minutes that I had been away, my seat had been taken by a large woman with two children, so there was nothing I could do except to explain the situation, and offer to take one of the children on my lap. The ice cream had to be shared equally between the two children, and I got very little of it. By now the bus was packed pretty tightly, and the luggage rack over our heads was perilously over-loaded. The floor of the bus, too, was suffering from the holiday crowds and looking in an awful mess. For a while there was a lemonade bottle dancing up and down on the floor just ahead of me. The people sitting nearest seemed quite oblivious to it, but it was driving me frantic with its constant journey to and fro. Eventually, I could stand it no longer, and I deposited the baby I was holding on someone else's lap, and collected the bottle and tucked it firmly down between the seat and the side of the bus. The litter problem that day must have given the bus company a big headache, and I fell to wondering about the poor women (or men) who clean out the buses – and also thinking there should surely be some sort of litter basket on the buses where the tidy ones could put their sandwich bags and toffee paper. In due course the crowd dispersed, and I was relieved of the baby who waved at me and blew kisses as she was firmly carried off.

I was now able to ask the conductor to sign my schedule, and made a note of the price of the ticket. The signature I have is of J. B. Lockwood and the fare was 10s 9d. The bus arrived at Carlisle at 8.50pm and M. Kilpatrick signed my card for me in neatly printed lettering, and told me that the distance from Glasgow was 113 miles. Both the conductor and the driver were interested to hear that I had reached John O'Groats safely and was now on my way home.

I found that the last bus for Keswick had left at 7pm, so I decided to go on as far as I could in the right direction, and was advised to take the 9.10 bus into Wigton. This was only nine miles away, with a fare of 1s 2d. J. Clark signed for me, and upon my enquiring if he thought I might get accommodation in Wigton for the night, suggested that I made a quick change of buses at Wigton and go on to Mealsgate where I could probably find a farmhouse where they took in guests. So at 9.35 I hopped off one bus and on to another about to make the quarter-hour's run into Mealsgate. The time was getting late; it was now 9.45pm and I kept my fingers crossed as I jumped off the bus outside a grey stone wall and approached a door across a wide courtyard. The house looked large and roomy, with a roof of dark tiles; nearby were a number of farmhouses and there were fields in the twilight beyond. I knocked several times, feeling a little fidgety in case my presence in the dusk might prove a bother to the occupants. I need not have worried as I was given a pleasant reception. They could put me up at the farmhouse, I was told, if I did not mind sharing a room with another woman – a niece. I was offered tea and nice ham sandwiches for supper. And this is how I came to meet Mrs Mary Lambert of Carlisle. We talked for some time before going to bed, and she told me that she was a corsetiere – a representative for Messrs Spirella – and that her job took her all over the place, fitting on corsets. We had an hilarious hour together while she initiated me into the mysteries of corsets – or should I say 'correct corseting' Mary? I was given a private demonstration on the exact way a corset should be put on; and shown the newest styles and most glamourous colours – peach pink being the height of luxury. Roll-ons and hookside – busk front – girdles and step-in – nylon satin with downstretch centre panel – I learnt about them all.

Mary was certainly a most vivacious talker and demonstrated her words most effectively. We continued our discussion in the morning until it was time for me to catch my bus, which fortunately for me meant only a walk outside the farmhouse. She also signed her name for me on my schedule for my overnight stop. When the bus came along, it was quite full! (I waved goodbye to Mary at least four times!)

'It's all right – you wait here,' said the conductor. 'This is the church bus, and I'll phone for another right away.' There were four of us waiting, and he was true to his word – another bus came along in 10 minutes and I got my favourite seat, up front on the top for my ride into Keswick. While waiting, I stolled up and down, and over a stone bridge. Under it ran a little stream, and the sunlight played on the rippling water and tossed the shadows of tall grass into the stream. So now it was Sunday, and I was back in England. The transition this time had been a secret, as I had crossed the border near Gretna Green in the evening light, and had scarcely been aware of it. I think my interest had been diverted by a large haystack that was on fire, and which filled the air with black smoke, and a pungent smell.

From Mealsgate to Keswick, the journey cost 1s 9d and my schedule was signed by another conductor who was interested in my journey. My schedule, being covered with signatures and notes of distances and fares, was enough to start most conductors chatting and they quickly showed enthusiasm. This time the signature was of R. Connell Stampery of Wigton in Cumberland, and I finally got into Keswick at 11.20am. This was an occasion for a mild celebration with myself, as I was up to scheduled time, and could now hope to put into effect an arrangement that I had talked about to a friend at least three weeks before.

We had agreed to meet in the Lake District on the Sunday afternoon of 31 July – the Bank Holiday Sunday, presuming of course that I had been able to get to John O'Groats and back into England in the time I planned. She would be on holiday then, and I now only had a short way to go to get to our rendezvous. This was to be at three o'clock on the little bridge at Ambleside, where the tiny house made of stone is perched high above the stream below. My time had been good, and I had an hour in hand at least before three o'clock. I had, in fact, time to dawdle a little, so I looked around Keswick after getting the signature – of J. Steel – beneath the Keswick stamp at the office in the bus depot. The floor of the office was covered with expensive-looking rucksacks, and my small blue shoulder bag looked a little tired against such swagger equipment, but as it was now proudly displaying a red silk band with the words 'Bus Riders' Club London to John O'Groats' on it, it seemed to hold its own with the hefty well-balanced waterproof bags of my invisible companions. I dumped it down and paid for it to be cared for in my absence, and wondered as I left it behind whether anyone would now connect me with such an adventurous journey, for without my shoulder bag I felt that I melted into the landscape and would pass unnoticed. My feet took me along the High Street among the holiday makers for a meal, and then back to the bus for Ambleside. I began to look forward to seeing my friend, and wondered whether she would be at our meeting place – I now knew its name: the old Bridge House that spans Stock Beck. Nearing Ambleside there was another general exodus, and it looked as if the bus would continue its journey empty. Conductor N. Carradus signed my schedule, fare 1s 10d. Ambleside was cheerfully crowded when I reached the bus depot and I was in good time. Again I dropped my shoulder bag in the office, and bought myself an ice wafer at the coffee stall – where I was thrilled to have them recognise me. I told them about my journey, how I had reached John O'Groats in five days from starting point near London, that I had really had a wonderful journey, and that I was here on the way back – taking things leisurely. I walked back to the bridge and sat on the coping stone within a few feet of the little house. I intended to be seen as this was our meeting place and my bright red headscarf should be noticeable too.

Some boy cyclists had pulled up and leaned their bikes near the bridge. We chatted and I told them where I had been and I must say that they listened very politely and seemed very interested. It was no use my looking for my friend, who would be in a car, so I had to hope that she would see me without any difficulty. She was on holiday with her relations from the Midlands and probably touring round for the day; I hoped that her arrangements would permit our having tea and a chat together. I need not have worried – in a short time a car moved slowly across the bridge, pulled into the side and I saw a smiling face looking towards me and my friend waving. The door of the car was opened and I got a frenzied welcome from a bonnie wee poodle when he realised it was me.

We had time for a good talk and a lovely tea at a hotel, and a run to the top of Troutbeck. This beauty spot was overflowing with visitors. Cars were parked with only a few inches between them. Dozens of people sat with their legs dangling over the edge of the road or rested on the slope of the grass. Below us there were sheep grazing, and in every direction there was a wonderful panorama of lilac brown mountains and green valleys. But the beauty spot was marred by crowds – it had almost become too popular! The wayside farms were blotted out with cars and bicycles and the little lanes were dangerous with traffic. There seemed at that moment to be more people on Troutbeck than anywhere else in the Lake District. My friends and I drove slowly round, seeing the beautiful views from the top with the lake below framed in the trees. Then we returned to Ambleside, back to within a few yards of the bridge where they had greeted me a short time before. I waved them goodbye, having promised to pay them a visit when I had completed my journey. The car disappeared round a bend in the road, and I returned to the bus depot for my belongings – my bouquet of heather and my blue shoulder bag. They both seemed a good deal lighter for the rest.

Chapter 13

A short bus ride to Windermere station and then I got off the bus and walked down the steep hill to Lake Windermere and the parish church which was calling people to Evensong as I passed. The holiday crowds had thinned out as I began to look for somewhere to stay the night. I knocked first at the home of Mrs Dent where I had found a room on my journey the previous week but I learnt from a neighbour that Mr and Mrs Dent were away, and I had to go elsewhere. I drifted up the hill to the right and made several enquiries before Miss Dulcie Barker took me in and made me welcome, and promised to fix me up for the night – if I came back later. 'Season's been the busiest I have known,' she said. 'But I'll make room for you somewhere.'

My arrival at Bowness on Windermere had coincided with August Bank Holiday, and I was in two minds what to do next. I could continue my journey southwards, in buses that might be packed to overflowing, or I could stay awhile and see more of the Lake District for another day or two before going on. Perhaps then the intense flow of traffic might have died down. True, it was peaceful and quiet by the lake, but the cars parked outside the hotels proved that there were a lot of visitors about, probably having dinner.

I wandered round the church and past the hotel windows. In one of them I could see some of the kitchen staff working. Nothing fascinates the passer-by more than to watch someone else working! I was no exception. The people moved round with ease and the atmosphere inside suddenly looked most inviting. I've always dreamed of working in a big hotel and I had an idea! A few minutes before I had been thinking that I should like to stay in Bowness for a day or two, but that my cash might run a bit low. Perhaps there was a way of earning something to cover my expenses – perhaps I could do a job – Perhaps?

I looked at the hotels again, and then – without another thought – decided to try at the one nearest the Lake. The gentleman who answered my polite enquiry looked a little aghast.

'For two days.'

'Yes, please – there's no fun in being on your own in a holiday crowd.' It's all I could think of to say. A poor excuse but it seemed better than none at all, just then.

'I'll ask Mother. Will you wait here?' I waited by the enquiry desk. A charming woman appeared and I found myself explaining my position quite truthfully. I told her about my bus journey to John O'Groats, and how I was now on the way home. I did not want to travel among the holiday crowds and my money was running short. She seemed to be amused at my story. 'Well, what do you think you could do?' she asked pleasantly.

'I don't really know, but I though there might be something I could do in the kitchen.'

'The silver needs cleaning! You could do that if you like,' She suggested. It sounded all right to me, and I thanked her. 'We start at half past eight, so you'd better come in at nine.' I walked back to the Lakeside in a dream. Everything had worked out perfectly and I'd get my meals as well, she had told me.

Miss Barker had made up a bed for me and I had for company a beautiful white cat who accepted my presence disdainfully. A table had been laid and I had a light supper.

Not daring to explain, I went out quietly in the morning leaving my coat and bag in the room and my heather standing in a bucket of water. I decided that I would probably have time at midday for explanations. I was at the hotel before nine, and was shown into a small coffee kitchen in which there were three people who made themselves friendly.

Silver teapots, cleaning cloths and Goddard's plate powder were placed on newspaper on a small table by a window. I began the work methodically. What is easy to one, is hard work to another, but at least I could soon see results. The silver teapots were removed bright and shining, to be replaced by coffee pots – dull and dirty. 'Wash your hands, and come and have breakfast!' someone told me. I thought a cup of tea wouldn't come amiss and joined others who were going through a long corridor to the staff dining room to have tea and something to eat. We were back in 10 minutes or so, to work on the coffee pots. 'Don't be long, there are the hot water jugs next,' I was told – 'And these butter shells.' Butter dishes shaped like little scallop shells toppled over with the height of the pile. They held glass bowls which held the butter balls.

'Could you do this tray?' asked an immaculate waiter, who had been darting in and out of the coffee kitchen during the morning. 'And mine too, please,' said another equally immaculate waiter.

There seemed no end to it.

'You go and get your dinner now,' a respite came with the lunch hour. Then it was back to the silver. All thoughts of seeing Miss Barker about my room had gone out of my head.

There must have been hundreds of pieces. Coffee pots, teapots, hot water jugs, butter shells, trays and at least one heavy ink stand from the hotel lounge. As fast as it came to the table where I sat, so it was cleaned and polished and rushed away again – I worked hard. All round me too, was the scene of intense activity.

'Four coffees, two coffees, six coffees' – so it went on for about an hour. The coffee pots were washed and drained, the china washed and rinsed and dried – and the things stacked away again.

But not for long.

Another call, and the tray was reset and the coffee disappeared towards the dining room or lounge. Here was the work and the workers! No time to talk, and less time to think. The waiters and waitresses in their smart black and white uniforms flashed back and forth through the open doors and along the corridors. The girls wore little aprons and caps that were quite pretty. Another lull, and I was offered another cup of tea. 'You'd better have it now, we get busy again soon,' I was told.

Busy hardly describes it – the atmosphere was tense, and the drill of getting the trays ready became a sharp staccato. There seemed to be about a dozen people rushing in and out, fixing trays and carrying them forth. They certainly took a great pride in the speed they could keep up. And all the time, I polished and the silver now gleamed on the trays as they were carried away.

'It was about time this silver was cleaned.' I heard someone say. 'It looks nice!' said another. And then, for the others in the room, came the washing up and clatter of crockery, a cleaning down of all the working counters, and a washing out of towels. I kept busy on the cleaning and polishing, but all the while my eyes were drawn to the antics of the 'tea boy' – a tall thin lad whose job it was to arrange the coffee pots and water jugs on the trays. His movements, which were quick and precise anyway became a kind of dance, and as the rhythm in the room got faster, so he too became even quicker until his feet sounded like a mad

typewriter on the floor. He moved like a thing possessed down to the shelves, then leapt high like a dizzy gnat in mid-air while the steam flew from the urn, then he paused for a second while the things were arranged on the tray before he leapt into action for the next ballet movement downwards to the shelves again. The atmosphere grew hot and pungent; smells of coffee and tea filled the air.

My head ached a little, and the people moving to and fro into the little room seemed like puppets, and the boy with the loose knees and flickering fingers kept the others racing to his tune. For over an hour the crazy rush was kept up, then as suddenly it ceased. The boy slumped a little over the table and the crowd dispersed.

I heard them go. Cars, one after another, pulled away from the front of the hotel, to gather speed as they moved past the lake. The invisible holiday makers that day became a collection of coffee and teapots on a tray and a fast moving scene that I shall never forget.

Down in the staff dining room where I joined others for meals, I spoke when I was spoken to, and avoided direct questions. It was quickly assumed that I had come to stay – to take the place of someone who had left – but I merely said that 'I was on the silver.' This explanation seemed to be accepted, and nothing further was said until I was advised to see someone about my room, and I realised that the staff slept on the premises. Not wishing to explain more than I could help, I thanked them, and wandered away to wash and tidy up.

By the end of the second day I had cleaned and polished 300 pieces of silver (counting the cutlery and pepper pots), earned myself a pay packet of £3, had all my meals and could have had a room too, if I had known about it in time, and was still among the magical beauty of the Lake District. However, I had to leave the haunting misty hills, and have the strength of mind to find the right buses and get back to London.

Miss Barker was very busy with her guests, so I did not have the opportunity of telling her what I had been doing. I repacked my bag tidily before going to bed so that I should be ready to leave in the morning, and stood the bucket with my heather in it near the door so that I would not be likely to leave it behind. It looked quite fresh for all its wandering, and I hoped that I should be able to get it back to London looking nice.

It was a lovely dark mauve heather, and seemed to carry with it a picture of the Highlands, from whence it had come. It was my only excess baggage – my very treasured souvenir, and I wanted it to keep as long as possible. Soon I was ready to go to bed, and I slept well – waking up when it was light to another beautiful sunny day.

Wonderful summer!

Above:
David MacBrayne took delivery in 1952 of a batch of Bedford OLAZ coaches with Duple bodies and varying seating capacities according to whether there was a mail or freight compartment at the rear and, if there was, its size. Seating in No 150 was 25. It is seen at Inverness waiting to leave for

Oban. *Edward Shirras*

Below:
Another of the 25-seat versions was 156 which is seen operating to Dores, a short working on the route to Foyers along the eastern shore of Loch Ness. *Robert Grieves*

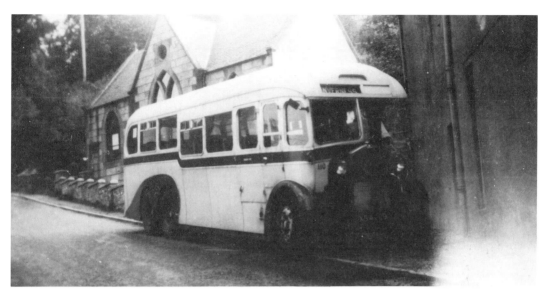

Below left:
On the route from Inverness to Fort William there was coordinated operation by Highland Omnibuses and David MacBrayne the former being heir to the services acquired by the British Transport Commission from MacRae and Dick in November 1951. Highland K87, illustrated earlier in Inverness garage is here seen in Invermoriston on its way from Fort William to Inverness. *Edward Shirras*

Above:
Still in MacRae and Dick livery but carrying Highland fleet number 110, this Cowieson-bodied Albion PR145 began its life with Young's Bus Service, Paisley in 1937 and was withdrawn by Highland in 1955. It is seen parked in Fort William. *Edward Shirras*

Below:
Bus operation at Fort William was largely a David MacBrayne responsibility and a substantial allocation of vehicles was made to the local depot. These were maintained smartly as exemplified by 94, a Park Royal-bodied Maudslay Marathon coach of 1948 together with 7, a Commer Commando with Glasgow-built Croft body of 1949. *Robert Grieves*

Photographed on a much gloomier day in Fort William with the pier in the background is an AEC Regal III of MacBrayne on the service to Inverlochy Village. *Edward Shirras*

Below:
Ben Nevis and Fort William. *Scottish Tourist Board*

Right:
Seen in Kinlochleven village, but travelling in the opposite direction to that taken by Mrs Leather, namely from Glasgow to Inverness, is MacBrayne 136, a Park Royal-bodied Maudslay Marathon of 1949 which was in fact the last such vehicle to be added to the fleet. It is now in the care of preservationists. *Robert Grieves*

Right:
Photograph of Mrs Leather taken in Glasgow by a news photographer.

Above:
Passing through Glasgow it was possible to see a large number of locally-built Albion Venturers in service with Glasgow Corporation Transport Department such as Roberts-bodied B83 which is seen in George Square en route from North Carntyne to Balornock.
Robert Grieves

Below:
Although not strictly relevant to Mrs Leather's journey, the Western SMT Glasgow-London service was at the time being operated by a fleet of Guy Arab LUF coaches with Alexander 30-seat bodies which had been new in the previous year (1954). Seen on the outskirts of Glasgow with a fine coating of snow on its front panels is FSD 464 (1086).
K. K. MacKay

Above:
The return journey from Glasgow to Carlisle was by Western SMT and by way of Kilmarnock and Dumfries. The Whitesands stance in the latter tended in the mid-1950s to present a varied selection of Western vehicles. In this view from the left are 1029 (GYL 375), a 1945 Guy Arab with Northern Counties body ex-London Transport; 831 (BSM 824), a Weymann-bodied Dennis Lancet II ex-Caledonian dating from 1936; 822 (GSM 125), a 1947 ECW-bodied Bristol L5G ex-Caledonian; and DL21 (CS 5269), a 1937 Leyland Tiger TS7 with Alexander body. *K. K. MacKay*

Below:
Going still further back – probably some 25 years – this view of Annan marketplace shows two Caledonian buses on the Dumfries-Carlisle route. The PLSC Lion facing the camera is bound for Carlisle while the LT Lion will head for Dumfries. *Robert Grieves Collection*

Above:
The last bus for Keswick had left when Mrs Leather reached Carlisle and it is therefore slightly tantalising to include this view of all-Leyland Titan PD2/12 KRM 259 (then numbered 310) about to leave for Keswick. The bus dates from 1951. *Edward Shirras*

Above:
Eastern Coach Works bodywork of the bus type on Leyland Royal Tiger chassis was not all that common but five examples were delivered to Cumberland Motor Services in 1952. One of these was numbered 326 but later became 153. *M. A. Taylor*

Left:
After Keswick came Ambleside where Ribble 2776, the last but one of 50 all-Leyland Titan PD2/3s delivered in 1950, is seen waiting to leave the bus station for Lancaster on the service from Keswick. *Edward Shirras*

Left:
The Ribble bus station in Preston, with, from the left, 2330 (RN 8986), an all-Leyland Titan TD7 of 1940 waiting to leave for Heysham; 1323 (DRN 263), another all-Leyland Titan but this time a PD2/3 built in 1950; and 2037 (RN 8602), a Titan TD5 of 1939 with 1950 Alexander bodywork bound for Chorley. *Ian Allan Collection*

Above:
Soon after Mrs Leather had passed through Ambleside on both northward and southward journeys Ribble undertook a substantial modernisation scheme. This view shows how it looked the following summer. *Ian Allan Library*

Right:
Ribble 298, the first of the Leyland-bodied Leyland Royal Tiger buses delivered in 1951, is seen on a short working to Leyland on the Preston-Leyland-Chorley route operated jointly with Fishwick. *Ian Allan Collection*

Above:
The last of the batch of Brush-bodied Leyland Titan PD1/As delivered to Ribble in 1947. For this posed photograph it is wearing the blinds for the service from Chorley to Preston. *Ian Allan Collection.*

Below:
A typical Manchester scene of the early 1950s with two Manchester Crossley-bodied Crossleys. Nearer the camera is 2091 a DD42/4 of 1948. The other is 2946 a 42/3 of 1946. *Alan Cooper*

Standing in Lower Mosley Street bus station, Manchester, waiting to leave for Derby in 1953 was this Harrington-bodied Leyland Tiger TS8. It was withdrawn in that year but a number of the batch were rebodied in 1950 and saw six or seven years more service. *G. H. F. Atkins*

Another Lower Mosley Street view but this time of a Trent Leyland Royal Tiger with Leyland coachwork dating from 1951 on the limited stop service between Manchester and Derby worked jointly with North Western via Macclesfield, Leek and Ashbourne. *G. H. F. Atkins*

Left:
Lowbridge Willowbrook-bodied Daimler CD650s were particularly associated with the Blue Bus Services of Tailby & George and with the service from Derby to Burton-on-Trent via Etwall on which this example is about to leave Derby bus station. *G. H. F. Atkins*

Below:
Five Brush-bodied Foden double-deckers entered the Derby Corporation fleet in 1952. 107 is seen approaching the marketplace somewhat later in its career when it was engaged mainly in peak hour duties. *T. W. Moore*

Bottom:
A demonstrator before it was bought by Burton Corporation in 1947, this Guy bodied Guy Arab III later passed into the hands of Stevenson of Spath. *T. W. Moore Collection*

Left:
When the postwar No 11 of Burton Corporation was bought in 1950 the Guy Arab III had a highbridge Davies body. It was rebuilt by the corporation in 1963 and saw eight more years in service before being bought for preservation.

Below:
The last of the Midland Red half-cab single-deckers to remain generally in service were the SONs with English Electric bodies dating from 1936 to 1939. When photographed in 1956 No 1933 was 20 years old.
G. H. F. Atkins

Bottom:
In this view of Stratford bus station the queue for the Midland Red bus operating the Birmingham service has left its marker and joined the bus hidden behind the Stratford Blue Leyland Titan waiting to leave for Shipston-on-Stour on the Oxford road. *J. F. Parke*

Chapter 14

I thanked Miss Barker for her modest bill, and for making me so welcome, and left after having breakfast.

The road up from Bowness on Windermere Lake is a bit of a drag, being both long and steep, but I had plenty of time so I took another look at the ivy-clad hotel where I had been working for the past two days before wandering past the gift shops and up through the little town. Everywhere seemed quieter – the main traffic had thinned and there were fewer people about. With one diversion and another it was nearly 11 o'clock before I was on the main road waiting for a bus to take me to Ambleside. I wanted to call at the Post Office there before resuming my journey – there might be a letter waiting for me from the family as this was one of the addresses I had left in case anyone might want to reach me. A post office is particularly useful to the traveller, and a post office savings account doubly so!

I was there all too soon, and was pleased to find four letters awaiting my call. I tucked them into my bag to read later and dropped by the coffee stall for refreshment and to say 'Cheerio' to the folks there before leaving.

'How long will it take you to get back to London?' they wanted to know. 'Well, it's nearly noon Wednesday. I shall be travelling the rest of today, all tomorrow, and I expect to be home about midday on Friday.' I told them. They thought it sounded 'Good going', to get so far in the time on local buses.

'I shall not hurry. I like to take it easy. I think to have time to enjoy things is a luxury in itself,' was my reply. We chatted for a few minutes more and then I left them. Whether you want to or not, you cannot help loving the Lake District, so I was in my element on top of the next bus out of Ambleside which runs all through the prettiest valley down to Kendal. The fare was 1s 3d and I considered it quite one of the finest pieces of lake scenery.

My schedule was out on my lap again – there were now six pages of it – and I asked the conductor to add another signature with the date. At Kendal where the big 'K' shoe factory is, I would need to change buses

in the town. The lakeland was now, alas, behind me, but the houses look quite interesting – often of white stone which is typical of Westmorland, and often too, they lie back to back on hilly streets in quaintly assembled communities. I was fascinated watching the enormous eight-wheeled lorries that were moving down the Penrith road loaded with heavy motor car equipment. Several came along at a time, so that they made a procession through the streets. Like me, they were going south and I wondered how many of them would be travelling the long road to London.

I did not think of them for long as my mind was diverted by the sight of a lovely butterfly, and the need of a quick cup of tea and a sandwich before getting the next bus. There were plenty of shops and a cafe or two in the main thoroughfare and I hurried into a clean looking place. Tea and sandwiches cost me 1s 6d and I made sure of a piece of wholenut chocolate to slip into my pack for the journey. There was no telling when I should get a better meal, and a bit of chocolate at the right moment will do wonders. I eat a lot of chocolate on buses!

There were queues for the buses everywhere and mine was no exception. I chatted with a woman near me for a few minutes while I waited for my bus. I went up to the top and took a seat at the back, and someone spoke to me. 'Do you mind if I sit with you?' asked a young man, 'I could not help overhearing what you were saying and I was most interested!'

This led to my having a companion for part of the journey from Kendal to Preston, and to my not taking much notice of the scenery. He told me that he was a student at Leeds University, and was spending his holiday in the Lake District. Part of the time he had been working in a big hotel to pay for his trip. He, too, had been in Windermere! You can imagine how I chuckled to myself, and I wondered whether he would be amused by my recent experience. After a while I told him, and we laughed a good deal and swapped our experiences.

'You got paid better than I did!' he said.

'That must have been because I work faster!' I said. Quoting the old nursery rhyme – 'But he got paid but a penny a day because he couldn't work any faster!'

I remembered to get a signature from conductor P. Hodgson when I paid my fare (2s 1d) and put the schedule safely back among my belongings. This was the fare from Kendal to Lancaster, and I later paid for a ticket to get me on to Preston.

'That's really something to be proud of,' said my young companion. 'Proof positive, in fact.'

'Yes, that's what I meant it to be,' I assured him, and he plied me with questions about my journey through Scotland.

Then he told me more about himself, and that he was studying bio-chemistry. He planned to work in a laboratory connected with the brewing industry and had to understand all about the mysterious processes concerned with brewing beer.

'We live and learn!' I said. 'I did not know there were any mysteries about beer!'

He gave me a few bits of information about yeast and fermentation. I told him that it was over my head and would have to be satisfied to leave such knowledge to the scientists, and the would-be scientists of the future, like him. So I have to thank Mr F. T. Joyce of Bolton for a very pleasant hour, and any knowledge I have about the brewing of beer. We ended our chat with a more serious discussion on money matters concerning travel and holiday accommodation, and I was able to give him the benefit of my experience. We both agreed that they were important things – travel in any shape or form helps to broaden the mind, and make you tolerant of the ideas of others. I did not see much of the scenery from this bus, but I do remember looking down while passing a field and viewing a strange sight – a fellow with an apparently expert hand with the scissors trimming another's hair, right in the middle of the field. They were quite oblivious to the curious glances from the people on the bus. No doubt they were a long way from the shops, or perhaps they could not afford to spend their hard earned money on haircuts.

I arrived at the busy town of Preston at half past three and decided to get a meal if possible. I waved goodbye to Mr Joyce as we parted company. I think he said he was going to Chorley.

I found a cafe open, and made sure of something substantial to eat. About half an hour later I made my way back to the bus station to see how I would be fixed for another bus. I thought I would be getting along, but the best laid plans of mice and men 'gang aft agley', as it is said and mine were no exception.

In the bus station, a lady recognised me and stopped to speak to me. 'I remember you,' she said. 'Weren't you going to Scotland by buses? – last week, it was, that I saw you?'

And so I told her about my journey and while we talked, another woman whom she knew, came up and joined us in the conversation and then a clippie and a bus conductor joined us, and soon I was talking of my journey to an interested crowd of bus drivers and conductors, and people who earn their living with the Ribble buses. It was only natural that the bus people would be interested in such a journey, and they were most enthusiastic, so I showed them my packet of bus tickets and the pages of signatures – which I called my schedule. I suppose they were mostly drivers and conductors who were off duty, but if one or another had to leave the group they called out to one another, 'Hey Bill – come and meet the lady who has been to John O'Groats and back here by buses!'

They were full of congratulations, and eventually they took me up to a little office to meet the publicity manager for me to tell him of my experience. He was interested in the mileage, and the amount it had cost, and asked me a lot of questions – 'How far in a day?' . . . 'Were you comfortable?' etc, etc.

I told him that my biggest difficulty had been in catching connections because the timetables had been made up without thought of the needs of a long distance traveller. He laughed and agreed that not many people would think of going such a distance, and that such a journey was an eye-opener to him. And so I chatted, and the time went by, and instead of passing half an hour in Preston as I had intended, I was there two hours and it was 5.50pm before I actually got a bus to take me on my way south again.

Holidays are unpredictable things, and the joy lies in not planning anything too rigidly, and so I can look back on my visit to Preston with pleasure, for I had found myself among friends.

It mattered little to me that I now had to jump two buses to get to Manchester as I went via Chorley and Bolton and arrived in Manchester at about half past eight. I must not forget the items on my schedule which read '3.30 Preston – J. Billington, arrival 5.50 Preston dep. Chorley 9d. E. Beckett. Chorley – Bolton 1s 2d B. Walmsley and Bolton to Manchester 1s 3d. J.U.'

This brings it up-to-date and finds me looking for a cafe or small restaurant in the deserted streets of Manchester. For deserted they appeared to be, as I went through the city, and round and round the shopping area in a bit of a daze. I was getting hungry, which was not surprising, as I had my last meal in Preston at about 3pm. It was my fault entirely, and I could not blame the buses. I had talked too much at Preston, and was now feeling exhausted . . . Except for small bars at the main bus depots, these north country towns are poorly equipped with cafes of the middle class type, and snack bars close early – so it is well to plan your meals better than I did on my return journey.

I enjoyed seeing Manchester with its big offices and shops and before I realised I was so hungry I had wandered up Oldham Street and across the road to the big glass-fronted office of the *Daily Express* where the lights were ablaze, ahd there were people working. I went in and saw the reception clerk and we had a delightful 10 minutes; and I returned to my quest for supper. Food seemed to be the one thing I could not find in Manchester for I could not go to the expense of a big hotel, nor would I have enjoyed it, but it was very necessary to get something. I went round Manchester for nearly two hours without finding anywhere, and eventually I appealed to a policeman who directed me to a Chinese restaurant where he assured me that I would be able to get a reasonably-priced meal. I admit I approached somewhat timidly – the neon sign directed me downstairs where there was an atmosphere not in keeping with a housewife-on-a-bus-ride, but the smell of fragrant coffee drifted towards me and I went to the nearest table .

A waitress switched on an amber light to see me better – or so I thought. Not daring to even look at the menu I asked the waitress if there was egg on toast, or fish and chips, and I also ordered some coffee. Just then I could have eaten a two-pound steak, and a dozen eggs but I was well aware of the state of my purse. The Chinese proprietor eyed me rather doubtfully from his little cubicle where he took the money as if I were an Eskimo. I need not have been so anxious. The food was delicious and the charge quite reasonable and in a little while I was sitting back comfortably in my seat and looking at the decorative walls, and feeling at peace with the world and very appreciative of the business-like quality of the oriental man behind the grille who had added more than he knew to my holiday.

It was quite late when I left the restaurant and I now had only one problem left – where to spend the night? I take things one at a time – you will notice – it never does to dwell on two problems at once. One is usually enough.

So I walked along the main road where I had met the policeman – as an easy way out. After a few minutes I found him trying out door handles to see if all were securely fastened up for the night, and thanked him for his help over the food question, and asked him if he could direct me to an address where I would be able to get bed and breakfast not too far away.

'You'll find the Young Women's Christian Association hostel just round the corner of Peter Street,' was his suggestion, and after thanking him again and giving him a short explanation why I was wandering about so late I followed his instructions and was soon settled with the lady warden (S. Gough) who led the way to clean sheets in a quiet room for the night. I hung up my bag and settled down. There was a bathroom, and when I came out I heard a voice asking me if I was 'coming down for tea?' I hardly wanted any, but it gave me the opportunity of speaking with someone so I followed the girl through corridors and down the stone stairs to the dining room on the ground floor. Sure enought it was possible to get tea and biscuits, so I joined the others and enjoyed a snack before 'lights out'.

All the problems of the day had been solved.

Chapter 15

Everywhere there was noise and bustle and for a few minutes after leaving the Peter Street YWCA, I wandered round just looking. I had been up early, and joined the others in a small queue for tea or coffee and scrambled eggs. There appeared to be about 16 girls and women and although few of them would have known each other the atmosphere was friendly. The bill was modest too and that cheered me up a lot.

Well, to continue, I enquired for the Lower Mosley Street bus station, and my schedule reminds me that I caught the Manchester to Buxton bus at 8.25am, for it was signed by A. Quayle on the top of my fourth page. This added another 24 miles, and my bus ticket cost 3s 2d. The journey took about an hour and a half and the bus stopping places along the road seemed like a piece of English poetry – Birch Lane, Hazel Grove, New Mills, Furness Vale, Whaley Bridge, Horwich and Chapel-en-le-Frith, Dove Holes, Peak Forest Turning and Buxton Market Place.

There were a lot of young people on the bus, laughing and talking together; they were evidently enjoying a holiday in the Peak District. The bus moved with the leisurely grace of a tortoise among the hills and dales that surround Edale Moor and the Peak, with Kinder Scout and Featherbed Top in the distance. The scenery varies in character between one county and another, and a photographer could find work for a lifetime in one county alone.

I did not go right into Buxton on this bus, which was due at 10.20, because I chatted with the conductor, and asked about the next bus for Derby. I could catch one at 10.10 at Cross Road, so I took his advice, was able to leave the bus before we got to the end of the journey and caught another for Derby to get me over another 37 miles. The Bakewell Agricultural Show was on, and the traffic was dense and moving very carefully. My ticket cost 4s 6d and the schedule was signed by Mr Harry Cutts. This was a very slow bus, stopping every 10 minutes through Bakewell (its tarts are famous) via Darley Dale, Matlock known for the Hydro; Belper, Duffield and Derby. There was plenty to look at and admire. In the Bakewell neighbourhood, people go to see Chatsworth – one of the local beauty spots and the

famous house – the home of the Duke of Devonshire. I was told of the most elaborately laid out water garden, but of course I did not see it. There always seems to be someone on the bus who knows about these things!

It was nearly 12.30 when we reached Derby, so I was looking forward to getting some lunch. The conductor told me I should have about three quarters of an hour before I had to be ready for my bus to Burton-on-Trent, so I made my way through a nice meal in the cafe at the bus station. Derby is a beautiful city with wide streets, well signposted and clean. The houses lining the streets look prosperous and the people had happy faces.

After lunch, I left Derby for Burton-on-Trent, as it was more convenient for the buses than going to Birmingham direct just then. This was at 1.15pm and the 12 miles cost me 1s 6d, and Mr T. Wells – the conductor – added his signature to my list. It was 2.20pm when the bus arrived at Burton, which is known throughout the world for the quality of its beer.

My bus for Birmingham went from another bus station at 2.30 – with the result I had an awful job to catch it. Not knowing the distance or that I could have caught a Corporation bus for a 2d fare, I walked and arrived breathless to find the bus I wanted about to leave.

It was very hot and I felt tired and dusty. I had vague hopes of getting a lemonade, or an ice cream before making another two-hour bus journey. However, luck was with me! An Inspector was standing in front of the bus, discussing something with the conductor. I checked with him the time the bus was leaving and asked if I would have time to get a drink?

'No!' was the reply, 'We're due out now.'

'And it's going to take me two hours to get to Birmingham before I'll have the chance to get a cup of tea!' I said.

'Yes, if you're going that far!' the conductor added.

'Far!' I said, 'I've already travelled from Manchester this morning,' and produced my schedule to prove it.

'You go and get your drink – We'll wait for you,' said the conductor, 'And anything else you want,' put in the bus inspector, 'Leave that schedule with me. I'd like to look at it.'

So I thanked them and left my precious schedule with the inspector while I hurried to the snack bar over on the other side of the paved courtyard – to a glass of lemonade and an ice cream.

'You've got some pluck!' commented the inspector when I returned, and he gave it back to me. 'I hope you've enjoyed it all.'

'I certainly have!' I told him, and you can bet that I meant it. 'I'd like to have a bash at a long trip like that, one day,' put in the conductor, as he jumped aboard and I took my seat. So we left Burton-on-Trent soon after 2.30, paid 3s 3d for the 29-mile ride to Birmingham – and the route lay parallel with the River Trent and through Lichfield Valley.

The roads got wider and busier as they approached the towns of the Midlands and at about 4.20pm the bus arrived in Birmingham. Just a two minutes' walk took me to the next bus for Stratford-on-Avon. It was too early for tea and as there was a bus in, I jumped on it and was soon on my way through the Forest of Arden – time 4.25pm.

This part of England is blessed with many rivers, and I enjoyed it. Next to me on the front seat on the top of the double-decker bus was a young man, who had a small attache case on his knees. He opened it to put in something he was extracting from the pocket of his coat. There was no room to lift an arm, so I moved sideways a bit.

'There is soft I am – to be keeping chocolate in my pocket.' the man said in little more than a whisper. 'No matter!'

'From Wales you are – and no mistake!' I laughed at his unusual turn of phrase. He opened the window in front of us.

'Melting it is, indeed! It's a shame!'

'That's a pity!' I agreed and he raised his hand to throw it away. Quite involuntarily I stopped him; not quite knowing why. It may have looked too good to waste, or it may have been that I did not like the idea of both chocolate and paper descending as 'litter' into the road below. I do not know.

'Most of it seems eatable – and it's whole nut chocolate too' I said, looking down at the packet.

'Yes, indeed! Would *you* like it now?' the young man said, and he unwrapped the chocolate slab for my inspection.

'Well, frankly I can't really see much wrong with it. Only a bit of it is melting.'

'You have it! You eat it before it melts away.' And so I had his chocolate, and he turned to the little case and found cake and sandwiches for himself. After saying thank you, we chattered awhile.

'You're going to Stratford, is it?' he asked me, and the Welsh intonation sounded like someone singing. 'Like a seat in the 'Gods' we have here.' He meant gallery. 'There is a better view than down in the stalls,' and he pointed towards the seats inside the bus. We were riding behind a heavy lorry the bus driver was making an effort to pass; but it was not possible so we joined the slowly moving traffic crawling along like snails. And the passengers sat patiently waiting for the bus to get a move on. The young man and I exchanged names, and he told me that he was on holiday. 'I'm on holiday too,' I said and told him about my bus ride. 'Indeed! And you go alone?' he queried, obviously amazed. 'Of course! Why not? I've been perfectly happy on my own. Although I have often had someone pleasant to talk to – like this.' I told him.

He sat silent for a moment, looking at me. 'Alone! And you with your years. You're not young, you know.' he said with Welsh outspokeness. 'I know . . .' I told him, sighing. 'I've been having a wonderful time. I've seen so much beautiful scenery that if I never see any more, I ought to be satisfied.'

And then he began to laugh, first quietly, and then as the thought that prompted him penetrated deeper and deeper, he laughed uproarously, until he shook with laughter.

'Indeed! I must tell them at home. – Afraid to go out, they are! Like mice . . . TIMID!' He was referring to his sister, or his wife – or mother, or all of them. I did not know and he laughed so long, that I began to laugh, too – and forgot to ask him.

'There is nothing to be afraid of.' I insisted. 'A woman today can go alone anywhere she wishes.' I told him emphatically.

'The courage! You have the courage. To be admired, it is!' said Mr Lewis Raffin. These were fine words, so I went on to tell him of some of my experiences. 'Faith you have – in your fellow men, good to see it!' he said.

'And why shouldn't I have faith?' I queried.

'A rare thing. You'll be writing a book, indeed,' he said.

'I should have plenty to say and I would not need any imagination, either.' I told him. 'I have truthful notes of the whole journey, but there would be no blood and thunder – just a humble description of my journey and bits about people like you.' Again he laughed but I do not think he discredited what I said. He finally spoke again. 'A determined woman. Yes, a determined woman!'

'You have to be very determined to keep to a bus schedule like I have. You have to know where you are going, and keep on until you get there.'

'Keep it hu-man!' he then said, and I wish I could write it just the way he spoke with the emphasis on the last syllable, and with the right degree of singing to the sounds of the words.

I paid for my ticket, and the signature on my schedule was from E. Beachus, and we arrived by the bridge at Stratford-on-Avon at half past five. Mr Raffin was kind enough to invite me to have tea with him at the Buttercup Cafe – so we had tea in the afternoon sunshine among the holidaymakers, who were at this cafe with its pretty sunblinds and coloured umbrellas over the tables. It was almost a continental scene it was so colourful and bright. We took snapshots for souvenirs before we parted beside the buses . . . Mr Raffin of Birmingham to look round Stratford-on-Avon and me to continue my journey towards home. I thanked him for his kind hospitality, and pleasant conversation as I left him.

I found I had just over an hour in Stratford-on-Avon so I wandered away from the bus station in several directions to see the shops and places that were near. The broad expanse of bridge over the Avon had attracted many people who stood in groups, leaning on the stone coping, and looking at the Shakespeare Memorial Theatre, or into the water at the swans.

My next bus, leaving at 6.45pm would take me around the upper reaches of the river, and through more lovely country to Oxford. Crowds had begun to gather near the bus stop, so I went into the queue to be sure of a seat on the bus. Two young women came up behind me and one of them asked me if I knew where she could get some rock with the words Stratford-on-Avon on it. As I had seen some in one of the shops I suggested that if she would take my bag and heather for a few minutes it would be quicker if I got it for her. She thanked me and I hurried off to the sweet shop. When I got back the bus was in, and the queue moving forward.

'We should have kept a seat for you!' said the one who wanted the rock. 'Yes, I felt sure you would.' I said, giving her the rock, and taking back my things. 'What a lovely bunch of heather, said the other. 'Where did you get that – not from Birmingham or Stratford-on-Avon, I know.'

'You're right about that – it's from the North of Scotland and it's a grand souvenir of my journey.' I said with the right degree of pride. 'You've been to Scotland,' she said. 'Aren't some people lucky?' she added, addressing her companion.

'Yes, and I've been by buses like this all the way there and back again.'

I think I enjoyed surprising people with this statement.

'Good heavens. What a journey!' We had all climbed to the top of the bus and seated ourselves near the front, and we continued to talk, and they told me that they had been to Shottery to see Ann Hathaway's cottage – and I learnt a little more about Shakespeare's birthplace and the surrounding countryside. I remembered to get my schedule signed by the conductor – as far as Long Compton – who was G. Lloyd. Here, the bus crew changed, but the same bus went on to Oxford; so I bought another ticket to add to my collection. The signature is in very faint pencil but I think it reads H. Arnold. We were in Long Compton at 7.38pm and had another 90 minutes journey to get to Oxford. Several Americans had joined in the conversation asking a lot of questions about the countryside.

By this time, I had exchanged names with my other two companions and learnt that they were Mrs R. M. Moody and her sister, who came from Abingdon. They asked me where I was going to stay the night as I had already told them I planned to stay in Oxford.

'Oxford's a busy place just now, you'll never get in anywhere.' Mrs Moody warned me. 'It doesn't matter, I'll find somewhere, or I'll take another bus ride along my way until I find a quiet village which looks hopeful.' I told her.

'If you don't mind another bus ride tonight, you are welcome to come home with us. We live out near Wick Hall, Radley, it will take another half an hour.'

'That's very generous of you, but I don't think I should put you out,' I said.

'You won't be putting us out as we have a small guest room and shall enjoy having you, and hearing more about your journey.' There was no point in my turning down their kind offer, so it was arranged. 'I am very grateful for the chance to stay with you,' I told them. 'You're going to save me a lot of trouble!'

'It's Thursday, so the local fish shop will be frying, and we thought of having fish and chips for supper. Will that be all right?' she asked me.

'Of course – a fish and chip supper will be very nice.' And I told them of my other meals that day – tea with Mr Raffin at Stratford-on-Avon – and breakfast at the hostel in Manchester. We did not lack for conversation, and we were still busy talking when the bus arrived among the spires of Oxford. We had passed Blenheim Palace near Woodstock. I had caught a glimpse of this historic place on my way up, but I did not know that it was the birthplace of Sir Winston Churchill, and that it had been built in the reign of Queen Anne in 1705. The gardens had been designed by Sir John Vanbrugh and Capability Brown and had been kept as a royal park since the time of Henry II. I made a note of the fact that the palace was open to the public during the afternoon – during the summer at a charge of 2s 6d. It has been called the Versailles of England, and this was praise indeed for the beautiful gardens of Versailles near Paris are known throughout the world.

We had not time to dawdle in Oxford, for Mrs Moody led the way to another bus which was due out in a matter of minutes. (It was just after 9pm.) I had enjoyed a long day of bus riding, but if I was tired, I had no time to think about it, and on this trip our journey was enlivened by the witty remarks of our bus conductor. I think it started when I bought my ticket and asked him to sign my schedule. 'I'm Uncle Tom to everyone,' he said. 'Will that do?' 'Well, I would prefer your name. That is, of course, if you have no objection.'

'What's it in aid of?' He asked. Mrs Moody laughed, and told him that I had been to John O'Groats by buses, and was now on *his* bus on my way home. He sat down as if the very sound of such an exploit made him gasp. 'I must hear more about this!' he said.

So I told him the story and explained that his signature would help to complete it.

'And you've been doing this all the way up and down the country. Have you enjoyed making yourself a nuisance?'

The other passengers were listening to us, and he kept on with his questions, pretending to be baffled at my insistence that I needed proof. 'Well, now let's look at those tickets!' So I showed him my collection of tickets and they had to be passed round. And he joked and teased and asked the passengers what they thought about him signing – and there was a chorus of 'Yes, you do!'

'All right let's have it! And now that I know all about it I should like to congratulate you on a very grand achievement because I can see that you will achieve your object. You've only another 50 miles to go.'

'Yes, I should be home sometime tomorrow. I haven't far to go – Reading, Maidenhead, Slough and home that way.' And I was pleased to notice that he had dropped his bantering tone, and was quite serious.

Meantime, one of the passengers who had been looking at my bus tickets, counted them up and made the number to date (60) and I added that the mileage would be about 1,400 by the time I got home. I did not know the accurate figure as this would be very difficult to assess,but the fare average per mile would help to fix the figure, when I finally counted up. I found everyone very interested, which gave me a good deal of encouragement.

By half past nine Mrs Moody told me that we would soon be at Wick Hall, and we gathered up our belongings, and said goodbye to the passengers who had been so friendly and to Mr C. F. Gorton (Uncle Tom) the jovial bus conductor. We were at Wick Hall at 9.40, and collected a fish and chip supper as we walked to Mrs Moody's home. A wash and brush up before eating, a saunter round the garden while it was light enough to see it – and Mr Moody came home from duty to join us. He was in the Berkshire Police,

and we all talked our way through supper and over tea and cake afterwards. This was my last evening out, on my holiday jaunt – tomorrow 5 August I expected to be home.

I had missed seeing Oxford, so I saw Abingdon instead, but I had heard the famous bells. You can hear them everywhere and they are a constant delight. There are Stainer's musical chimes at Carfax, the bells in Magdalen Tower, and the boom of Great Tom. With so many church bells they form a unique orchestra. They are so much a feature of Oxford that as well as being called the City of Spires, it is sometimes referred to as the City of the Bells. I cannot leave Oxford without a word about its delicious chunky brown marmalade, made from an old family recipe belonging to Mrs Frank Cooper which was made at Oxford by Frank Cooper Ltd. Finally I must mention the publishers of Bible and prayer books – the Oxford University Press which has a large printing works there.

Morning in Abingdon was bright and sunny – the weather I had had all the way, with scarcely a cloud in the sky. I had a leisurely breakfast and bath, and helped Mrs Moody to tidy up in the kitchen. To keep my schedule right, Mrs Moody signed it for me – my 14th overnight stop. She told me that she did a parttime job as a telephone receptionist at a switchboard in a hospital, and we would have time to walk into Abingdon together where she would see me off on my bus to Reading. I collected my heather and bag, and we left the house. 'Write and tell me that you've got home alright, won't you?' she asked me. 'Yes, I will,' I promised, as I thanked her for her kindness to me. 'I've loved having you, and I wish you luck on the last stage of your journey.'

'It's nothing now – just a few hours and I'll be home,' I said.

'Nothing!' said Mrs Moody. 'A lot of people would think the journey from here to Reading sufficient of a bus ride. It will take you two hours, you know!'

'I did not know, but two hours will seem like nothing to me!' I insisted.

Chapter 16

'Yes, I suppose you're right. Well – good luck and goodbye then – Here's a No 50 bus coming.' The bus pulled up by a red bricked building in the lovely town of Abingdon, and I waved goodbye to my new friend. I had promised to send her a little painting I had done from a picture of Ann Hathaway's cottage so I made a note of this to remind me. I knew that the moment I was home there would be plenty of jobs to keep me occupied and the note would help to jog my memory.

This journey from Abingdon to Reading cost 3s 9d, and as the bus left at 10.35am we would be due at about 12.17, and I would get lunch somewhere before going on. The bus crossed a bridge over the River Thames and I settled back in my seat for the leisurely run towards the river where it flows between the Chiltern Hills and the Berkshire Downs.

My precious schedule was looking the worse for wear when I presented it to the conductor who kindly obliged with his signature. The name I have is of G. Billing, who told me that he came from Wallingford. The weather was ideal for early harvesting and I took an interest in the fields on this journey – the superb colour of the golden wheat brightly shone like silk, and the vivid poppies growing here and there beside the hedges, standing after the corn had been cut.

The bus moved like a grand duchess – majestically. For sheer restfulness, nothing could beat it. I day-dreamed the rest of the morning away through Clifton Hampden, Benson, Wallingford, Moulsford, Streatley, Pangbourne and Tilehurst into Reading. The villages are attractive and beautifully kept and there is an abundance of water. Such beauty shows up the dull ribbon development of the new towns that give one an ache in the heart. Often the villages lay far from any highway and the buses ambled around to pick up passengers from the remoter districts so rich memories of our beautiful countryside remain with me.

In one place, swans drifted down a stream, followed by a string of fluffy young ones to make a sublime backwater picture. In another, the cottage gardens were so full of flowers that they overflowed into the lane and a drift of white cerastium or a few colourful nasturtiums announce the presence of a little cottage

behind the hedge. A big bumble bee buzzed into the window near me, and must have travelled a mile or two before he floated out to continue his work among the flowers.

The bus stopped outside several inns along the road and riverside. The names of the pubs were delightful: the Waggon and Horses, the Plough, Bull, Crown, Roebuck and many called the Swan. I loved the old brick-built houses best – they were something to marvel at. Chatting with an old man whose face was wrinkled and weathered by wind and sun I learnt something about the building of these old cottages. But I think that it was thatch that started it. 'Ee be puttin' a new coat over the ault waistcoat – ee be,' said the old chap. I laughed, and then I saw that there were two men doing the job – one on the outside and the other whose arm and head could only be seen – as something that looked like a long needle came through.

'Looks as if he is sewing it on!'

'That's so too! Tarred rope ee be using with them spics o' hazel.' The 'spics' looked like hefty hairpins that were being pushed into the straw by the outside man.

The bus moved on and our picture of the rare craft of thatching went out of sight behind us, but the old man and I went on chatting for several miles. 'Bricks be better,' he said. 'Thatch is awk'ard for fire. Dry weather like what we been 'aving may set a thatch a-fire, and it's 'ard to put ee out y' know!' I agreed with him about that, and he went on again about bricks. 'Give me bricks ev'ry time – not that old straw,' he muttered.

'You may be a builder then?' I questioned politely.

'Naw – not 'zackly that, but I've done a bit of building in me time.' So we talked of bricks . . . pink bricks, yellow bricks – red or white bricks until I gave up trying to keep up with him. Bricks, it seemed, could be made of – or with – anything. They could be thin or fat, common or stylish, heavy or light. It wasn't long before he had to leave the bus, and a country way of talking went with him. He got out by an old country pub probably to have a pint of ale and a bit of bread and cheese. He disappeared immediately and there was nowhere else he could have gone so quickly.

I could see for miles as the bus moved over yet another bridge across the river. Did all that water flow on to Westminster – past Richmond and Putney for the Boat Race? And now, because of the old countryman, I began to take note of the herringbone brickwork between the timbers of some of the older houses. Much simple pride must have gone into the making of such an attractive frontage, or it may have been a note of luxury in cottage economy.

At the next stop a young woman came out of a small house to catch the bus, and in looking at her chestnut brown hair I nearly missed a lovely Dutch barge with its side flippers moored near a weeping willow tree. It was a lovely sight. The conductor evidently knew the girl, because he greeted her with 'You got the morning off Doris?'

'No – I'm only a couple of hours late. Mum's not well,' she said, her cheerfulness suggesting that there was nothing seriously wrong with her mother.

'And how's that young man of yours?' he asked.

'She grinned as he gave her a ticket. 'Oh! he's all right. You take too much interest in my young man!'

'Well, I'm looking forward to seeing your wedding.'

'You will. I've no doubt of that.' and then she appeared to address me. 'Thinks he owns us! Just because we met on his bus!' she said with a laugh.

'That's nice anyway. Nice of him to take such an interest, I mean,' was my reply.

'It's no use my being on my dignity,' she added. 'Peter does nothing but talk about me to everybody.'

'And Peter is the young man, I suppose.'

'Yes, we usually travel on the same bus to Reading together. He works at a shoe shop, and I'm in the hairdressers,' she told me.

'That's the secret of your hair, isn't it? It's a most unusual colour,' I added. The girl continued to chat and I enjoyed listening to her. She was pretty, and seemed to have plenty of confidence.

'You said that you met your fianceé on the bus, didn't you?' I asked, when we had talked for a while. 'How did that happen?'

'Oh, Pete gets on at the stop before me, and on that particular morning he was still standing on the platform when I wanted to jump on, and the conductor said to him 'Now then young Peter, make way for a lady. She's got to get to work too.' And then he helped me on the bus, and before we knew it we were talking about everything under the sun. My Peter's as wide awake as anything. You just couldn't be alone long when he's around.' The girl laughed.

'And were you alone, before?' I asked.

'I suppose I was, but it was different – I wasn't grown-up and did not expect any boyfriends,' she said.

'Well! you'll look like a queen at that wedding.' She smiled and turned to gaze out of the window. I was afraid my compliment had made her shy, but in a moment she had returned to the conversation.

'Peter says that I shouldn't be shy, but then he puts everyone at their ease.'

I smiled as I thought of Peter. We had travelled through Pangbourne, Purley and Tilehurst and were now on the outskirts of Reading. I gathered up my things ready to get off. We should be at the bus station near the railway stations fairly soon.

'I hope you have a day like this for your wedding. It couldn't be nicer, could it?' I said.

'Well, we might. It's only a month away, – so perhaps the sun will still be shining.' She pulled out a little mirror from her handbag and found her lipstick. 'I might meet Peter. He sometimes goes to lunch early!' she said as if in explanation as she applied the lipstick. But the station was almost empty as the bus slowed up, and she got off. We waved goodbye to the conductor as we walked to the wide pavement.

'My golden coach!' she said, and I thought I knew what she meant.

'And mine too!' I added, although I knew she would not know what I meant. We said goodbye, as we went on our own way. I went towards a cafe, and she turned to cross the road and I saw the glint of chestnut hair bobbing up and down, as she disappeared through the traffic. There was no need for me to hurry and I thought I had better make sure of some lunch first. There was no difficulty, there were plenty of cafe restaurants, so I chose a pleasant-looking place with plants in the window and went in. It wasn't crowded, as it was about 12.30. I sat near the window and picked up the menu when my eye caught the glint of red-gold hair and a blue skirt on a girl who was passing. Sure enough it was my acquaintance from the bus; she moved to the edge of the pavement to cross the road and it was then that I noticed Peter – for surely that must have been him . . . a bronzed young man in a dark blue suit who had caught her arm to pilot her across the road. A sudden shaft of sunlight caught the top of both young heads. I might have been mistaken but from where I was sitting it seemed as though there were now two red-gold heads and two equally happy people. I hope the sunshine was a gentle omen of a radiant future for them both. They looked such a pleasant couple. They disappeared into the crowd as I ordered a lamb chop, runner beans and new potatoes – a lively lunch to end my eating out on this trip! The runner beans were particularly delicious. I had raspberries and cream afterwards. I had enough money for my last few bus fares when I paid the bill.

My next point was Maidenhead. The buses left from the open square at the railway station, and there was a half-hourly service. While in the station yard I had a chat with Inspector Hurn whom I had seen before. This time I thought he might be interested to know that I had almost completed my journey, and before I got on the bus he was kind enough to congratulate me and sign my schedule. The time was about 1.30pm and before I forget it, I had better mention that my fare to Maidenhead was 1s 8d. My ticket was pushed into the rubber band, a fat little collection which I thought was well worth keeping. Now the bus turned east towards Sonning and Twyford, where the lazy river flows; so although I could not often see it, this was still quiet river country and I could return to my window pictures of old churches, country barns, rose-covered cottages and views of the Thames Valley. I dozed a little for there was no one on the bus to talk to – or maybe I had eaten too much! It took about an hour to get to Maidenhead through Sonning Halt, Twyford, Knowle Hill and Littlewick with several other stops on the way and we eventually pulled up in Maidenhead bus station. I looked for the inspector I had met on the way up, but unfortunately he was not there so I talked to Inspector Benny instead. He was kind enough to give me his signature and to report that I had arrived in Maidenhead at 2.20pm prompt. The gulf between this lovely riverside town and my home near Twickenham had still to be bridged and in many ways they are worlds apart, although the distance would only be about 16 miles. For Maidenhead is still 'country' to us while Twickenham is a crowded dormitory suburb of London. Between the two lay the Thames Valley and the precious water course that has given life to hundreds of industries from Slough, along the Bath and Great West roads into the city of London.

My route lay due east, about two miles north of Windsor, with the playing fields of Eton in a sheltered spot between. You could not see Eton College from our bus, but it was possible to see the round tower and flagstaff of regal Windsor Castle from several points along the route. Maidenhead to Slough on a double-decker bus also gives a chance to see Taplow and Burnham Beeches – well known for the lovely beech trees. Now I was beginning to look towards home – the sky in the distance was hazy with smoke from chimneys and the roads were wide and full of traffic. I was out of the quiet backwaters and into the main stream.

Considerable skill was needed to handle the bus, demanding full concentration. Lorries, cars, bicycles, motorbikes and vans vied with each other for the crown of the road; and many a handful of people waited in groups to cross at vantage points. The small houses had a suburban flavour, each with its gabled front and narrow lawns. How everyone must love flowers, for there was not one plot without its flower beds and rose bushes.

The bus stopped at what had recently been a field. Weeds grew waist high, but not many yards beyond the weeds was the half-built structure of a house. Stacks of bricks and roof tiles crushed the weeds in several places, while an assortment of planks and scaffolding poles lay around. An ice cream van had pulled up near the site and brick–layers and builders, stripped to the waist and looking like Comanche Indians, were gathering around the van to get the cooling taste of ice cream. The noise of the traffic quietened down and I heard a workman whistling a popular tune as he came into sight shouldering a long piece of timber. The bus moved on, as I cast a wistful glance at a group of fragile red poppies and tall white daisies about to be mown down by a timber lorry backing into the field.

A plane roared overhead, evidently circling to land at London Airport (Heathrow) a few miles to the east of us. Another followed on the same course and I watched it as it went round, over the bus, throttling down the engines and quietening down as it flew.

It had become terrifically hot in the bus and I looked for more windows to open. My arms were red-brown and freckled and the reflection from car tops and passing windows hurt my eyes. I had lost my sun glasses. A wasp buzzed around on one of the window frames searching for a way out so I moved my hand away from the opening and gently pushed him into the air. Like us, he looks for freedom and will buzz in panic if he cannot find it. He soon disappeared from sight.

Into Slough High Street where a clock showed me that I would not have long to wait to get the 3pm out of Slough for Hounslow. Conductor P. Mowbray had been kind enough to add another name to my list of signatures and the ticket joined my collection.

From here, my journey would run through the level land of West Middlesex, where agricultural produce and especially good fruit has been grown. The route continued past London Heathrow, which is fast becoming the centre of a new kind of town housing the workers connected with the aircraft industry. The level land that grew wheat, beans and delicious strawberries now houses the giant airliners. They come and go all day long and seemingly half the night. It is on my doorstep, so I know it well.

On a bus driving past, you have no difficulty picking out aircraft for New York and you can see various types waiting on the tarmac. The road past the airport teems with traffic, bringing in passengers and workpeople, as well as cargo – and it is a veritable fairy land of lights at night. The bus stopped several times before we left the airport behind on the way to Hounslow bus station. A few minutes later the bus slowed down and we were soon going into the garage area.

I thanked the conductor, and walked towards the traffic office in the hope of finding Inspector White who had signed me out when I left on my journey – but Inspector E. Parker was on duty, so we had a little chat, and he signed instead. Now for my last bus which would draw up in the High Street, a few hundred yards away from the depot.

Though it is almost in London, my home town of Whitton has grown in the past 80 years from a tiny village round Whitton Park; and even now the important traffic which speeds on its way to Heathrow airport one way, and to Piccadilly Circus the other, has to come through the old village and past cedar trees which were planted in 1725. Whitton is in the postal area of Twickenham and is famous for the Rugby Union ground, and for turretted Kneller Hall, built as a home for the artist Sir Godfrey Kneller; it is now the headquarters of the Royal Military School of Music. Delightful concerts are given in the grounds during the summer months – and it is not unusual to hear a fanfare of trumpets echoing through the stately trees during a morning rehearsal – the same fanfare that was sounded by the trumpeters for the Queen's Coronation. We are also near enough to enjoy Sunday walks in Richmond Park, Kew Gardens and Hampton Court.

There was not much traffic today from Hounslow to Whitton in the middle of the afternoon – and the 33 bus only stopped at the village brick and stone church on the way. My daughter was christened and married there, and everyone loves its pepperpot tower and air of quiet simplicity.

My final bus ticket went into the rubber band and the last signature was crammed into the quarter of an inch of space left on the cardboard schedule. Conductor J. N. Fender (N.11469) had completed the evidence of my journey by service buses to and from John O'Groats.

I had been away a fortnight, travelled approximately 14,000 miles, spent £8 16s 7d on bus fares and had 64 bus tickets – and a million memories. The bus pulled up within sight of Kneller Hall, just before 4pm and I alighted. I felt proud of my achievement, and sent a wordless vote of thanks to all the bus drivers who had contributed to the safety of my journey.

A two-minute walk up our tree-lined road, and I turned the key in the lock. 'Anybody home?' I called, as I usually did, but there was no answer. I picked up letters from the mat and glanced at the dust on the hall table; then went through to the kitchen to lay my heather on the sink. My mind saw a picture of that heather amid the pine trees of Scotland.

Tomorrow, my daughter and her husband would return from their own holiday. I filled the kettle and put it on the gas to make myself a cup of tea. My holiday was over; I was home – HOME WITH THE HEATHER.